THE DEMOCRATS AND LABOR
IN RHODE ISLAND

THE DEMOCRATS

AND LABOR

IN RHODE ISLAND

1952-1962 / CHANGES IN THE OLD ALLIANCE

by Jay S. Goodman

BROWN UNIVERSITY PRESS, PROVIDENCE, RHODE ISLAND   1967

98058

Designed by David Ford

Type set in Linotype Caledonia

Printed on Warren's University Text
By Crimson Printing Company

Bound by Stanhope Bindery, Inc.

TO ELMER E. CORNWELL, JR.

ACKNOWLEDGMENTS

This book is a revised version of my doctoral dissertation for the Brown University political science department. The original field research was carried out during 1964/65, the present revisions between November, 1966, and February, 1967. What remain from the dissertation are Chapter I and Chapter II, both of which have been revised; all the other chapters are new. Chapter IV ("The Legislators") draws heavily upon my article, "A Note on Legislative Research: Labor Representation in Rhode Island," which appeared in the June, 1967, issue of *The American Political Science Review*. The editors of the *Review* have graciously given permission to include much of the same material here.

I am deeply indebted to a number of organizations and individuals. During 1964/65 I enjoyed the luxury of a year of uninterrupted research thanks to the support of the Woodrow Wilson National Fellowship Foundation. Some seventy Rhode Island politicians, labor leaders, and close political observers were kind enough to permit me to interview them, and they shared with me their many insights into the state's political processes. I cannot violate their confidences by naming them, but without their co-operation and expertise in party–labor relations, there could have been no book.

Acknowledgments

I was fortunate to have academic guidance of unusual perspicacity. Professor Elmer E. Cornwell, Jr., advised me with patient wisdom from the first germ of the research in 1963 through the construction of the book manuscript in 1967. Professors C. Peter Magrath, Erwin C. Hargrove, and the late Klaus Epstein were good enough to read and comment upon an earlier draft. From their knowledge I greatly profited; however, the responsibility for whatever errors remain is mine.

Dean Walter Kenworthy, of Wheaton College, was another source of encouragement and support. Mr. Joseph Benoit, the librarian of the *Providence Journal*, was of incalculable assistance in locating the newspaper material which is the basis of Chapter II. Mrs. Helen Durant, of Wheaton College, typed revisions of the manuscript with skill and without complaint. More than most academicians, I was dependent upon the loyalty, good cheer, and intelligence of my wife, who contributed all of these qualities unfailingly.

CONTENTS

TABLES AND GRAPHS

THE DEMOCRATS AND LABOR
IN RHODE ISLAND

I / THE FRAMEWORK

Why does one study state politics? As state government becomes more complex, such research becomes interesting for its own sake.[1] Further, research on state politics is relevant to the "theoretical understanding of influence in political settings of all kinds."[2] Finally, what happens in the states may well apply to national politics. What happens to labor–party relations in Rhode Island should allow speculation about the relationships of these groups at the national level.

The major theoretical concern of this book is the extended interactions of an interest group and a political party. While there are many books by political scientists on groups and parties, and some studies even relate the two, few analyze group-party relations in one setting for an extended period.[3] (Fay Calkins considered alternative labor strategies and party outcomes in five separate settings; the work of Oliver Garceau and Corinne Silverman analyzed one issue during a single legislative session; and John C. Wahlke and his collaborators reported upon the attitudes of four sets of legislators during one session.)[4] This study extends the sample population backward in time to encompass the ten years from 1952 to 1962 and focuses on a single state, Rhode Island. The primary concern is the phenomenon of change in group relations, but a number of other areas are also explored.

The Rhode Island Setting

For the social scientist Rhode Island provides an urban setting for research, a base with some relatively distinctive and some relatively common demographic and political characteristics. Only forty-eight miles long and thirty-seven miles wide, Rhode Island is the country's smallest state. Its population in 1950 was approximately 790,000, and it had grown to 850,000 by 1960.[5] Small size affected its political culture. Citizens expected to have easy access to officeholders, and face-to-face communication was possible at all levels.[6] What might be called political intimacy seemed to be part of the normal process of political participation.

Rhode Island was also the nation's most densely populated state, and over 80 per cent of its people lived in urban areas.[7] Forty-one per cent of the work force was engaged in manufacturing, making the state seventh in the nation in this category.[8] In other words, within its narrow boundaries, Rhode Island was a heavily urbanized, industrial state. Further, within this framework, Rhode Island resembled its New England neighbors in possessing numerous ethnic groups. Rhode Island ranked second only to Massachusetts, with 40 per cent of its people in the foreign-born or first-generation-American categories.[9] As each new group settled in the state, its members sought entry into the political structure. Their assimilation into politics—in pursuit of recognition and material benefits—brought them into conflict with the Yankees and also with each other. Often their battles took place within the Rhode Island Democratic party.[10]

Media can be important in the politics of any state. Rhode Island was unique in that one newspaper company, publishing the morning *Providence Journal* and the afternoon *Evening*

Bulletin, achieved effective state-wide circulation and dominated the state. These two newspapers gave exceedingly detailed coverage to local news, perhaps more thorough than
any of the major American dailies. As a result, civic and
political activists read them especially closely. Interest-group
and political-party leaders used them to communicate with
each other by releasing detailed press statements and reports
of their private sessions. Activists in Rhode Island were extremely sensitive to the treatment they received on both the
news and editorial pages of the *Journal* and the *Evening
Bulletin.* The two papers took a "good government" outlook
toward local affairs and a Republican position on issues which
could be placed in a partisan context. Their influence on activists is as difficult to measure as their effect upon voters, but
their combined daily state-wide circulation of 158,000, their
extensive local coverage, and their role in intergroup communication certainly put them in a strong position.

Rhode Island's politics were much like those of other states
in some ways, especially voting patterns. In the thirteen Presidential elections after 1908, Rhode Island voted with the
national winner eleven times, missing only with Hughes in
1916 and Smith in 1928. In the latter instance it was in line
with its neighbor Massachusetts.[11] Thus, in voting behavior
the state followed national trends. Party fortunes also paralleled
national politics. In Washington the Democrats achieved office
with Roosevelt in 1932, while in Rhode Island they won with
Theodore Francis Green as governor.

Green built a local coalition modeled on Roosevelt's and
with a similar composition. Green was backed by members
of ethnic groups, whose attendance at the polls was obtained
by rapidly developing urban political machines. Support for
the Democrats came also from economic groups in the population; in Rhode Island, as in the nation, labor was one element
in the new victorious coalition.[12]

During his second two-year term, Green consolidated the

5

support of the Rhode Island Democratic party. He forced passage of significant welfare and labor legislation, and reorganized the state government to give the party control of the judicial and executive apparatus. After Green's tenure the Democrats held the governorship for all but four years until 1962. Republican power during the intervening years was concentrated in the state Senate until the 1950's, when Senate control swayed back and forth between the two parties. But by the late 1950's the Republicans found that they could capture the governorship by nominating a candidate with strong personal popularity. The Democratic majority in the House of Representatives antedated Green, and its size increased steadily, reaching a peak in the mid-1960's. Students of state politics classify Rhode Island as a two-party competitive state.[13]

Rhode Island Democrats also developed a political style resembling that of the national party. At the top, in the 1930's, was a Yankee patrician adept at practical politics. The passage of fundamental reform legislation in significant quantities occurred simultaneously with the development of a huge patronage organization. For many people the party meant jobs. Murray Levin, observing the same phenomenon in Massachusetts, labeled it "personal politics," a style that relies upon "close personal ties between a mass of low-income constituents who desperately need jobs and state legislators who will grant them in exchange for votes."[14]

Interest Groups and Political Parties

Group membership and group political activity are pervasive characteristics of American life. Individuals join groups from motives ranging from a wish for comradeship to a desire for economic advancement. Meanwhile, as American society has become more complex, more and more groups of varying kinds have found it necessary to participate in politics to pursue certain goals. Organized labor, in fact, traces its contemporary strength to political events—it was released as an important economic force by the Wagner Act of 1935.[15] Jack Barbash wrote: "The growth of unionism that followed the election of the Roosevelt administration to power is a result of the favorable climate created for union organization in a positive and energetic way by government." [16]

Like other groups, labor has participated in political action, seeking to achieve its goals within a set of widely accepted informal rules of American politics. These rules rest upon tradition and acceptance; they are part of the political culture. One canon is that groups work through an intermediary organization, the political party, rather than by seeking direct control of government. Labor parties, like third parties generally, have been rare in America. Another canon is that labor use the regular parties in a democratic manner; the radical direct-action or subversive wings of the labor movement have almost always been hard-pressed minorities.[17]

American political scientists have been interested in groups since Arthur Bentley wrote *The Process of Government* in 1908. Bentley's group approach was revised by David Truman, who published *The Governmental Process* in 1951. As an upper-range behavioral theory, the group approach has its supporters and detractors.[18] This study avoids the controversy over the proper scope of group theory because it is concerned only with a limited subsystem, the labor–party relationship in Rhode Island. For such a restricted and clearly delineated study, even the critics of group theory would probably concede its usefulness.

Some parts of group theory do form important underpinnings for this study. One group-theory proposition, that group relations in American politics lead to major political results, can be accepted without question. So can the group theorists' explanation of the division of internal authority in private groups and their listing of the variables affecting external group operations. These aspects of the literature deserve some elaboration.

Truman defined an interest group as "any group that, on

the basis of one or more shared attitudes, makes certain claims upon other groups in the society for the establishment, maintenance, or enhancement of forms of behavior that are implied by the shared attitudes." When such a group makes claims "through or upon any of the institutions of government, it becomes a political interest group." [19] Truman cited four internal factors that affect the potential external influence of interest groups: (1) the degree of cohesion among the group's members, (2) the group's expectations of permanence, (3) the internal division of authority, and (4) the formal values that the group members share.[20]

By "internal cohesion" Truman meant the degree to which members give loyalty to one group and exclude competing claims for their support. The greater the internal cohesion of a group, the more likely it is that the members of that group will resist divisive appeals, and the greater the group's external bargaining power will be. The emotionally charged unions of the 1930's were highly cohesive organizations. Party politicians then and now assess the amount of rank-and-file support that labor leaders have and even the degree of solidarity among the leaders themselves.

"Expectations of permanence" are the attitudes of group members and those outside on how long an organization is likely to be in existence. These attitudes affect those within and without. Leaders of a group expected to be permanent arouse one set of reactions in politicians; leaders of a temporary organization generate different responses. Leaders of a group with reasonable expectations of permanence develop patterns of action and goals for themselves that differ from those of group leaders who want to settle one issue only. Leaders of new groups are frequently under greater pressures to obtain results than are those of stable, established organizations.[21]

The question of internal division of authority, of who rules, is an issue much debated since Robert Michels propounded his "iron law of oligarchy" in 1911. Michels said that the nature of organizations made internal rule by only a few individuals inevitable. Even an organization committed in principle to internal democracy would eventually have an internal oligarchy.[22] Many scholars have examined American labor unions for evidence of internal oligarchy or democracy, and Michels has had supporters and critics.[23] However, even those who accept the picture of widespread internal oligarchy are completely unsure as to what the external effects of the condition are.[24] Internal division of group authority affected this study only indirectly because in Rhode Island the AFL, the CIO, and the merged AFL-CIO, formed in 1958, were all organizations made up of representatives from other organizations. All of their personnel were leaders of other groups. The internal processes of rank-and-file–leader relations within individual unions are not touched upon.

Of course, the internal division of authority within the state-wide organizations themselves is relevant. A few activists, often the full-time officials, can control the political relations of a state organization just as they can those of a single union.[25] This possibility will be examined in this book.

One other aspect of internal division of authority is significant for this book. Writers on labor in America have suggested that the style and personal power of leaders whose organizations were created by a federation of existing groups will probably be different from those of leaders whose groups created their member units themselves, from the top down.[26] The latter leaders are said to possess more centralized power. This distinction appears to explain some of the structural differences between the national AFL and CIO, and to suggest some possible differences between their Rhode Island counterparts as well.[27]

A group's formal values affect the political options that it feels it may legitimately exercise. A labor organization committed to democratic procedures will act differently than one that believes officially in direct action. Within the democratic

9

rules, political action for the AFL has always meant something different from what it meant to the CIO. The AFL has always been committed to business unionism, a narrow set of economic goals. The CIO has had a broader social philosophy. This difference affected the conception that each group had of the proper degree and form of political action, and politicians were quite aware of the distinction.

Political parties are groups, but they are not identical with interest groups. A party is a clientele-oriented organization. Professor Samuel J. Eldersveld observed: "In contrast to the bureaucratic [interest-group] model, the party is almost by definition an open, personalized system." [28] A party, unlike an interest group, must conceive of its existing and potential support in the widest possible terms. Further, a party fulfills more diverse functions than most interest groups. Because parties actually manage government, they aggregate as well as articulate interests.[29] They resolve issues as well as present them while "representing and exploiting multiple interests for the achievement of direct control over the power apparatus of the society." [30] As an intermediary group collecting and satisfying the demands of other social units, the party must construct coalitions to achieve its own ends. Thus the party will tolerate and try to stabilize internal conflicts among its various groups of supporters. The Democrats in Rhode Island, for example, tried to harbor the potentially antagonistic small-business interests alongside organized labor and the upwardly striving Irish along with the recognition-seeking Italo-Americans.

The structure of party leadership also differs from the allocation of authority within the typical interest group. Although Rhode Island's state labor organizations were more congeries of ambassadors than hierarchically controlled groups, there were, nonetheless, identifiable lines of authority. Party leadership, in contrast, can hardly be visualized at all within an hierarchical model. Because numerous elements within a party possess independent power and the ability to exercise authority, the over-all division of authority is best described as "stratarchical." [31] Eldersveld explained that "such allocation of command and control to specified 'layer,' or 'echelon,' authorities is a pragmatic necessity. The very heterogeneity of membership, and the subcoalitional system, make centralized control not only difficult but unwise. . . . the party develops its own hierarchical patterns of stratified devolution of responsibility for the settlement of conflicts, rather than jeopardize the viability of the total organization by carrying such conflicts to the top command levels of the party." [32]

In talking about the strata of a political party, Eldersveld had in mind the layers of party officials—precinct workers, ward committeemen, and county committee members. For this study, the two relevant strata within the party are the legislative party and the executive party. The former is comprised of the legislators, their constituents at the district level, and the district party leaders who control their nominations. The latter is made up of the governor, his staff, patronage officials in the executive branch, the state-wide voting public, and the state party committee. These strata have some common interests, some divergent interests, and various authority relationships among themselves.[33] A secondary interest of this study is the patterns of leadership communication and coordination between the legislative and executive party strata.

Whatever the means used to hold the Rhode Island Democrats together, they must have been relatively effective because the party's external behavior, at least as it was measured in terms of legislative voting, was highly disciplined. Observers have noted the high level of party cohesion in the Rhode Island General Assembly.[34] After programs were agreed upon within the party, it acted so as to closely resemble the responsible party sought for so long by some American political scientists.[35]

Interest groups and political parties establish relationships with each other in ways that are easily described. Important direct communications take place in meetings of the leaders. These leaders bargain with each other, since bargaining is "a form of reciprocal control among leaders." [36]

Throughout American society bargaining is a major process in the allocation of political values. Successful bargaining presupposes a kind of social pluralism, the existence of multiple centers of power within the system; it also requires that there be sufficient agreement on rules and values for the bargainers to be willing to negotiate with each other. Thus, bargaining resolves specific points of contention against a background of consensus on fundamentals.[37] Leaders bargain "because they disagree and expect that further agreement is possible and will be profitable—and the profit sought may accrue not merely to the individual self, but to the group, an alliance of groups, a region, a nation, an unborn generation, the 'public interest.' " [38]

The labor leader is accustomed to bargaining—in internal politics, in contract negotiations, and in relations with other organizations. His political counterpart, the politician, "is above all the man whose career depends upon successful negotiation of bargains." [39] The labor leader has multiple goals. He wants specific political gains—favorable legislation. He wants direct political rewards—patronage jobs. He wants recognition of his status in the community—deference. In return, labor organizations offer multiple benefits to party politicians. They offer workers and funds for campaigns, and votes at elections. They provide support for party policies that may not affect them directly. And they give deference to the politician as an individual in recognition of his importance to the community at large.

The Hypothesis

The hypothesis of this book is that the relationship between the Democratic party and organized labor in Rhode Island has undergone a fundamental change in the direction of lessened labor influence. Three corollary propositions are: (1) major elements in the party have come to feel that they can achieve their goals without depending upon labor's support; (2) organized labor has become dissatisfied with the prospects of obtaining what it wants through the party; (3) labor has sought to establish its independence from the old, automatic alliance.

This hypothesis has considerable potential significance. The Democratic victory in Rhode Island in 1932 depended upon a tacit coalition of supporting groups; throughout the New Deal era the coalition solidified into a more formalized network of relationships and exchanges of benefits. One important group in the alliance was labor, which became especially important in Democratic victories after 1936. The labor–party coalition rested upon a harmony of interests obtained through implicit and explicit bargains among the participants; yet there is no reason why any political alliance should exist indefinitely in the American system. It may become impossible to arrange bargains equally satisfactory to all parties. Writers on the subject rarely specify under what conditions an alliance may deteriorate, nor is there any accurate record of such a situation from the perspectives of the various participants. This study aims to add to the record and at the same time to inquire whether the alliance of the Democratic party and labor, seemingly one of the closest in American politics, is destined to be something less than eternal.

What kinds of research findings would tend to verify the hypothesis? On the simplest level evidence would appear in the public record as to the course of labor–party relations. More important would be the perceptions of the participants themselves. Since people act on what they perceive to be real, the participants' perceptions would deserve the closest attention. Expressed dissatisfaction suggests conflict; perceived change allows the inference of real change. Interest-group leaders might be more inclined to verbalize dissatisfaction than politicians, whose tendency would be to minimize conflicts, but a difference in perceived satisfactions from the perspectives of labor and of the party would itself suggest an altered relationship. Successful coalitions require agreement on the terms and outcomes of co-operation. Perceptions of political reality should be very similar if group relations are to remain viable. If the groups have differing versions of what their relationship has produced, then one consequence would be frustration for one side while the other operated as if all were well.

A symptom of diverging perceptions would be a difference of opinion about how adequately each organization produced the benefits that it offered to the other in return for co-operation. Labor leaders and party leaders would disagree about what each gave and what each got. For example, the labor leaders might feel that their loyal support was not properly rewarded with legislation, or that politicians did not show appreciation of their importance by giving them proper deference. Politicians, under exactly the same circumstances, might believe that, considering what labor did for them, labor got more than its proper share of legislation and respect. In either case, how the participants felt they were served would determine their appetite for future collaboration.

The Research Strategy

The research strategy in this study was to examine the labor–party relationship from different perspectives: that of the public and that of each discrete set of activists. In the process information was also sought about the activists that would be relevant to understanding their roles in state politics. Accordingly, with the exception of Chapter II, which relies upon a written public record, the bulk of this book derives from 76 interviews conducted in Rhode Island between November 1, 1964, and April 1, 1965.

There were six categories of interviewees, encompassing the major participants in the labor–party relationship. (A seventh set, of observers, was also interviewed; newspapermen, labor lawyers and advisors, and gubernatorial staff members were included in this group.) A different questionnaire was used for each category, but some questions were repeated for more than one set.[40] Questions were asked about each respondent's background, about the internal processes of his group, and about the patterns of interaction between his and the other group. Then the respondents were asked questions designed to reveal their perceptions of, or attitudes toward, various aspects of the labor–party relationship.

The six categories of major participants were:

1. Labor executive board members—respondents who were on the AFL, the CIO, or the AFL-CIO executive boards for at least part of the 1952–62 period. Names were drawn from the AFL and the CIO board membership lists for the time prior to 1958 and from the board of the merged organization subsequently. When those who were more active in some other category were removed from this population, the number of individuals remaining totaled 61. From these a sample of 27, weighted for tenure and for the proportion of AFL to CIO members in the state-wide labor population, was drawn. Twenty-five of the 27 were actually interviewed. Labor executive board members were thought of as being activists at a middle-management level in the labor movement. They had considerable internal responsibility, their views were taken seriously in labor councils, and their time was devoted to labor; their public visibility was minimal.

2. Labor legislators—respondents who had some connection with labor and were also elected as Democrats to the Assembly for a minimum of one term between 1952 and 1962. Their association with labor, as ascertained from their biographies in the *Manual*[41] of the Rhode Island General Assembly, was that they obtained a livelihood from blue-collar work,

held union office, or listed membership in a union. Many of those who listed membership in a union were no longer engaged in the trade represented by their union affiliation; they had entered the professions or gone into business. Yet, since these legislators still listed union connections, it seemed reasonable to include them in this category. Labor lobbyists would certainly seek to utilize a legislator who advertised his labor background. A labor legislator was seen as an individual halfway between labor and the party. Which side he identified with and what his perceptions would be were matters of considerable interest in the research. Between 1952 and 1962, there were 30 individuals who fell within the category of labor legislator. From these, a sample of 16 weighted for tenure was drawn, and 15 were actually interviewed.

3. Democratic legislators—respondents who served at least one term as Democratic representatives in either house of the Assembly between 1952 and 1962. They listed no labor connections in their biographies in the Rhode Island *Manual* nor were they part of the elected party leadership in the legislature. They were, thus, the rank-and-file party legislators; as individuals they probably did not greatly influence party policy, but their views on the labor–party relationship were taken as indicative of the perceptions of a basic layer of political activists. Out of a population of 123 Democratic legislators, a sample of 16 weighted for tenure was drawn, and 15 were actually interviewed.

4. Democratic legislative leaders—respondents who were elected party leaders in the Assembly. Six of those interviewed served in this capacity between 1952 and 1962, while the seventh interviewed attained formal leadership responsibility subsequently. There were three individuals who served but could not be interviewed—two had died and one was exceedingly aged by the time of the research. The leaders were seen as party middle-management individuals whose say on certain policies was considerable, whose views and perceptions

were those of the cold-eyed professional politician, and whose authority might be greater than their low public visibility would indicate.

5. Labor executives—three respondents who held office in the state-wide labor organizations and a fourth whose informal authority was so great that the study would have been incomplete without him. These individuals were seen as the top decision-makers within state-wide labor, who also represented labor to the public and to political leaders.

6. Political executives—two respondents who served as Democratic governors of Rhode Island between 1952 and 1962. Within the party they were the most important individuals; they symbolized the party to the public; they negotiated directly with leaders of labor.

II / THE PUBLIC RECORD

This chapter, which is drawn almost entirely from open sources, primarily newspapers, provides information about events and people, and also a background against which the interview data can be evaluated. In re-creating the public record, some points have to be emphasized at the expense of others. The items selected pertain to labor's efforts to obtain legislation, appointments, and deference from the Democratic party and also items showing the party's responses. Newspapers are more likely to report conflicting situations than routine harmonious relationships among groups. Still, the Rhode Island public record is replete with material relevant to this book.

Halcyon Days, 1952–1958

The year 1952 began with Governor Dennis J. Roberts' annual message to the Rhode Island General Assembly. In his speech the Governor conceded that the state had very high unemployment compensation and workmen's compensation rates.[1] These rates were important because Rhode Island also had the nation's highest ratio of unemployed persons.[2] The *Providence Journal* attributed the continuing loss of textile jobs to jurisdictional disputes between the state AFL and CIO.[3] Roberts responded to the situation by proposing an industrial development corporation. The AFL reacted immediately by assigning three of its vice-presidents—Thomas Kearney, of the Electricians Union; Edward Quirk, of the Teamsters Union; and State Senator Frank Sgambato, of the United Textile Workers—to help Roberts.[4] The secretary-treasurer of the AFL, Edwin C. Brown, also made it known that his labor organization would agree to revisions of workmen's compensation and unemployment compensation if claims judges acceptable to it were appointed to review boards.[5] Brown suggested several prospective judges to the Governor. At the same time the AFL was working for a four-point legislative program to achieve a uniform state salary schedule for schoolteachers, higher cash sickness benefits, assignment of the Department of Employment Security to the Department of Labor, and a one-dollar-an-hour minimum wage.[6]

While the AFL was co-operating with Roberts, the CIO was quarreling with Democratic party leaders in the Assembly. CIO officials, upset by legislative rules and committee practices, were publicly critical of the House majority leader, James H. Kiernan, and the Senate minority leader, Raymond A. McCabe. The AFL supported the CIO in this dispute only to the extent of opposing final all-night Assembly sessions.[7] These sessions were so hectic that only the party leaders could keep track of the proceedings. As a result, they had control over all information and were able to have almost any item passed or defeated.

Nonetheless, in October the CIO Political Action Committee issued a blanket endorsement of Democratic candidates for state and federal office for the coming election. Simultaneously the CIO outlined an extensive list of programs that it favored: the creation of a consumer's council to investigate trade practices; an increase in workmen's compensation benefits; a one-dollar-an-hour minimum wage; a study commission on an unemployment compensation law; more regulation of public utilities; bargaining rights for municipal and state employees; an industrial development corporation as proposed by the governor; federal reinsurance of state unemployment compensation plans; reform of rules, longer sessions, and higher pay for legislators in the General Assembly; a new Milk Control Board; an end to racial discrimination; and a state rent-control program.[8]

Just as the 1953 legislative session began, the CIO president, Frank Benti, attacked the Assembly rules that allowed committees to kill bills. "He charged that the 'present system' permits the political bigwigs to dictate what is and what is not in the public interest, gives them control over added patronage, strengthens their bargaining positions with lobbyists and allows them to wield influence far out of proportion to their true stature in party councils and in their local communities." [9]

The CIO did, however, join the AFL and representatives of industry at a meeting with Governor Roberts to discuss changes in workmen's compensation and unemployment compensation. All agreed on the need for new legislation, and both labor and industry were willing to support Roberts—as long as he cleared new proposals with them before the proposals were introduced.[10] In February a group of CIO leaders met privately with Roberts for several hours to discuss labor's legislative aims. Roberts called the CIO's ideas "a good solid legislative program that would benefit the state's overall economy." [11] He also denied that filling the post of Deputy Director of Labor, which had been sought by the CIO since it had become vacant nine months before, had been a subject of his talks with the CIO representatives. The CIO was reported to want the appointment in order to balance the influence, in the Roberts administration, of the AFL president, Arthur Devine, who was Director of Labor.[12]

As the 1953 legislative session continued, Roberts held other meetings with labor leaders. The AFL asked him for an annual raise of $728 for all state workers; the CIO requested a five-man review board in workmen's compensation cases.[13] The CIO also publicly criticized the state Senate; it was unhappy with the Democratic minority leader, Raymond A. McCabe, and with the Republican majority members.[14] At the same time, labor's political energies were also consumed in a struggle between the AFL and the CIO over the post of Deputy Director of Labor. The CIO accused Arthur Devine of being unfair to CIO locals in labor disputes and of issuing too many holiday work permits to employers. Seven CIO officials complained directly to Governor Roberts, who re- mained noncommittal.[15] Roberts was visibly close to the AFL; he had been the major speaker at its state convention.[16]

Early in 1954 Governor Roberts appointed Edwin C. Brown, of the AFL, to the State Board of Education; his position was unpaid but prestigious in the community. In February Roberts denied a statement by the *Providence Journal* that his bill compelling public utilities to pay part of the cost of the agencies regulating them had actually been drafted by the CIO.[17]

The AFL and the CIO came together briefly to back Rob- erts' Industrial Injury Commission, which was opposed by busi- ness,[18] but then they resumed quarreling with each other. On May 7 it was made public that the Governor had offered Brown the post of Deputy Director of Labor as an attempt to counterbalance the appointment of CIO official John Bello to the Workmen's Compensation Commission.[19] The CIO vice- president, Thomas Policastro, protested against the AFL's being offered the two top positions in the Department of Labor.[20] To keep peace, Brown refused the appointment. By October the two labor groups were able to come together again to sponsor a television show endorsing Governor Roberts and urging citizens to elect Democratic majorities to both houses of the state legislature. Brown and Miss Elizabeth Nord, a CIO Textile Workers Union official, "criticized Republican office seekers and urged labor to support Democratic candidates."[21]

The 1954 election brought changes. In the legislative sessions of 1952, 1953, and 1954 there had been very little labor legislation. In 1955, for the first time, the Democrats could muster a majority vote in the state Senate because the tie between the parties could be broken by the vote of the Democratic lieutenant governor. Committee chairmanships in the Senate also passed to the Democrats when Frank Sgambato, senator from North Providence and full-time organizer for the AFL United Textile Workers, became chairman of the Labor Committee.

Changes were also taking place within the labor movement. Frank Benti, the CIO president and a personal associate of prominent Democrats, died. He was replaced by Thomas Policastro, who was closer to Lawrence N. Spitz (a brilliant labor intellectual and the Steelworkers' regional subdirector) than to any politician.[22] Policastro was also from the Steelworkers, a union with a history of political activism, ideological orientation, and increasing power in the state and in the CIO.

Although Policastro's first public statements were conciliatory toward the AFL, co-operation within labor did not follow. The AFL worked closely with Senator Sgambato, who watched over its bills in his committee and introduced many of its proposals along with ones that had originated with Arthur Devine in the Department of Labor.[23] But Sgambato became involved in a conflict with the CIO when Governor Roberts appointed Elizabeth Nord to Benti's former post on the review board in the Department of Employment Security, a post customarily given to a CIO member.[24] Senate Democrats refused to confirm the appointment, and the CIO accused Sgambato of causing the logjam.[25] Sgambato was alleged to be holding up the appointment in order to force the CIO to concede the post of Deputy Director of Labor to the AFL.

Miss Nord's appointment was delayed for three months before finally receiving approval.

The CIO's struggles were not confined to jobs. Although the CIO secured passage of its bill to make arbitration clauses judicially enforceable, its minimum-wage proposal was defeated, and a bill for a people's counsel, who would represent the public at hearings for fixing utility and medical rates, was blocked. Some of these difficulties may have been the result of too-extensive lobbying and overdetailed demands. The people's counsel bill finally died, apparently because the CIO refused to accept a proviso of Senate confirmation. The CIO wanted its own attorney, Julius Michaelson, to receive the $12,500 appointment and feared that he would not be approved by Sgambato. It therefore engaged in fervent activity: "Throughout the night, more than a score of CIO members walked the corridors, hoping to influence legislators into passing the bills they wanted. . . . Lawrence N. Spitz, CIO steelworkers official and lobby leader, sat at the side of Speaker Harry F. Curvin on the House rostrum when the people's counsel bill was tossed into the House judiciary committee to die." [26]

For the AFL, however, the 1955 session was an unparalleled success. Of the 21 bills that it backed 16 were passed; all of the 10 that it opposed were defeated. The AFL's annual legislative report stated that its lobbyists had been "cultivating good will among the members of the General Assembly, civic groups, and the public at large." [27] Among its successes were bills providing that employment advertisements placed by struck plants must indicate a dispute was in progress, that the Department of Labor could collect back wages for an employee, and that unions could sue for wages on behalf of members in state courts. A larger number of labor bills was passed in the 1955 session than in any other session in Rhode Island history.[28]

During the summer of 1955 the national AFL and CIO

were moving toward a merger. In Rhode Island the AFL president, Arthur Devine, said that he would like to head a merged state organization.[29] Roberts praised Devine publicly.[30] When the national organizations did merge in November, the state affiliates were given two years to work out their own terms for merger. Holding up the merger in Rhode Island was CIO opposition to Devine. Led by Lawrence Spitz, the CIO was said to feel that Devine was too tied to the Democratic party, too inclined to put the party's objectives ahead of labor's goals.[31] AFL leaders, on the other hand, said that they were happy with their political relationships; they saw no conflict between serving labor and serving the Democratic party.[32]

During 1956 there was major legislative controversy over the minimum-wage bill. Roberts proposed eighty-five cents an hour; both labor organizations supported a one-dollar-an-hour minimum. CIO officials described Roberts' plan as "unrealistic" and "a travesty." [33] The CIO president, Policastro, claimed that Roberts had failed to consult labor, but after the House passed the one-dollar-an-hour minimum-wage bill, Roberts indicated that he was willing to accept it. In the Senate, however, some Democrats defected, and a ninety-cent-an-hour compromise was finally reached. Some leaders, unlike the CIO officials, were openly happy with the outcome.[34]

By late April the efforts of the state AFL and CIO to merge were still snagged. The CIO insisted that the president be a full-time, salaried official who would be prohibited from holding any political job. This proviso ruled out Devine.[35]

At the same time the two organizations were going in different directions politically. The AFL endorsed Sgambato for the Democratic nomination for the lieutenant governorship, while the CIO supported John A. Notte, Jr., for the position.[36] By September the CIO was deeply involved in political activity. It backed three candidates in the Democratic primary, and over Republican protests, it invited only Democrats to its

Labor Day picnic.[37] Senator Sgambato was pointedly not invited to the picnic, at which Governor Roberts and John A. Notte, Jr., now the endorsed Democratic candidate for the office of secretary of state, were the main speakers. President Policastro, of the CIO, planned to provide 150 cars and 200 workers on election day to guarantee that all of the 25,000 CIO members in the state voted.

Labor's assistance, however, could not save the Rhode Island Democrats. The state voted for Eisenhower, and in that sweep the Republicans regained control of the state Senate. Roberts was returned to office by a margin so narrow that only a court challenge of absentee ballots kept him in. This "long count," over the day he was inaugurated, ruined Roberts politically; from then on the *Providence Journal* referred to him as the man who had to have voters disqualified in order to keep his office. Pressed on all sides, Roberts could do little for anyone. During the 1957 legislative session only one important labor bill was passed; it raised the minimum wage to one dollar an hour. The CIO publicly expressed disappointment.[38] Roberts chose the CIO's Labor Day picnic to hint that he would run again for re-election in 1958; on that occasion he also denounced his Republican adversary, Christopher Del Sesto, and the *Providence Journal*.[39] As the year ended, the two labor organizations were still unable to agree on the terms for a state-wide merger.

In January, 1958, the CIO indicated its approval of Governor Roberts by inviting him, but not his declared primary opponent, Lieutenant Governor Armand Cote, to its annual convention; the only other political figure to speak there was John A. Notte, Jr.[40] On March 19, Arthur Devine resigned as president of the AFL, while keeping his post as Director of Labor. He said that he had acted because of "attacks of the local press" and "certain political office seekers"; however, there were rumors of pressure from Roberts, who faced a hard election campaign and was embarrassed by labor's feuding.[41] On March 20, the AFL and the CIO announced that they had agreed to merge.[42] The Rhode Island AFL-CIO officially came into being on September 6. Policastro became the president; Edwin C. Brown received the only full-time salaried post, that of secretary-treasurer. Under a new constitution no officer or executive board member could hold a political position.[43]

In October Policastro called together 60 state labor leaders to plan strategy for precinct work during the campaign. At the same time, support was pledged for a special legislative session that Governor Roberts was convening to iron out the "merit-rating" problem. Roberts had often been criticized by industry and by the *Providence Journal* because, under the system of employer payment into the state's unemployment compensation fund, all employers were taxed at an equal rate, with no allowance made for employers who maintained stable work forces. Large employers who had a low turnover of employees wanted to be rewarded with reduced rates, but labor opposed this principle on the ground that the fund would be endangered if merit-rating were adopted. During the regular legislative session, the split between labor and industry prevented the passage of any bill. The special session was Roberts' effort to save his image, and during it he worked out an acceptable compromise. The principle of merit-rating was accepted, but was not to go into operation until the fund had reached an arbitrarily set level—a level so high that no employer could expect a reduction in rates for years. Labor was happier with this result than was industry.[44]

Shortly before the election the new AFL-CIO formally endorsed 21 Democratic and 3 Republican candidates for the Assembly. It endorsed all of the Democrats running for state office, declaring that "we believe most of the Republican candidates have been carrying on a political campaign designed to turn back the clock on labor and social legislation." [45] The AFL-CIO also said that Roberts had been "harassed by an opposition press and an irresponsible anti-administration segment of Rhode Island industry," but had, nonetheless, offered dedicated leadership and had "continually improved the economic life of Rhode Island." [46] The AFL-CIO leaders were attacked by the Republican gubernatorial candidate, Del Sesto, who called them "machine politicians" whose sole concern was the "reelection of Roberts"; Del Sesto accused them of "fostering an anti-business and anti-industrial attitude in the state." [47] The labor leaders replied by calling Del Sesto antilabor.[48] Labor's help was not sufficient for Roberts to win the election; he lost by 6,230 out of 346,780 votes. The Democrats did, however, recapture the Senate. In December Policastro announced that labor would work for a state income tax and a minimum wage of $1.25 an hour.[49]

Stormy Days, 1959–1962

At a January, 1959, AFL-CIO meeting the outgoing governor, Roberts, was presented with an office chair by the state's labor unions.[50] The gesture was symbolic because it soon became clear that labor had fewer political prerogatives than before. The new governor, Del Sesto, appointed a lawyer without labor experience to the post of Director of Labor; despite the AFL-CIO's objections, the Democrats in the state Senate rapidly confirmed Del Sesto's choice. Edwin Brown said: "If labor were as all-powerful as some of its critics try to make it out to be, it would not have failed to get someone from the ranks of labor appointed state labor director last week." [51]

The AFL-CIO proposed a program of 32 items for the 1959 legislative session. It gave priority to bills for a state fund for workmen's compensation; adequate lunch periods for public-school teachers; and improved working conditions for barbers, firemen, and musicians. It also took a strong stand for a fair-housing bill.[52] But progress was exceedingly slow, and in April labor leaders held an urgent meeting with the

Democratic legislative leaders. Two weeks later the AFL-CIO held a special Sunday afternoon meeting for 200 local union officials; at this session the state labor leaders proclaimed labor's independence of all political parties. Only 2 of the 32 bills proposed by labor had been passed in the Assembly during the current session. Furious, the labor leaders said that the only policy to adopt was a return to Gompers' philosophy of rewarding only friends. A Steelworkers Union official said that the Democrats had forgotten that they were the party of the workers, while a Painters Union leader claimed that the Assembly Democrats were all in the employ of the insurance companies. Bitter attacks were launched upon influential Democratic State Senator Francis P. Smith of Woonsocket. The AFL-CIO officials were also unhappy with the House Labor Committee, whose chairman, Thomas P. McHugh, was an Electricians Union agent.[53]

In reply Smith called Policastro "King Louis XIV . . . a conceited, pompous ignoramus who acts around here as though he were chairman of the Democratic party." Without Roberts, Smith maintained, labor no longer had "the front office to pull the chestnuts out of the fire." [54] Two reporters for the Providence *Evening Bulletin* commented: "On the surface, the bitter exchanges represented a personal feud involving three men. But underlying the personalities was mounting friction of broad character that had been clearly evident on capitol hill in recent weeks. . . . Labor leaders have become increasingly irritated at the General Assembly's slow action on their legislative program and legislative leaders have shown rising resentment at labor pressures." [55]

The politicians, likewise, had their grievances. They were displeased with what they regarded as unfair pressures from the Steelworkers Union during the fair-housing vote, and their pride had been hurt when the AFL-CIO president, Policastro, who was a Steelworkers Union officer, had refused to come to a Jefferson-Jackson Day dinner.[56] In the middle of May the old allies sat down again for talks; present were seven AFL-CIO leaders, Lieutenant Governor Notte, and legislative leaders. They held a give-and-take conference on labor legislation, legislators, and labor tactics.[57] Still, at the end of the session the AFL-CIO secretary-treasurer, Edwin C. Brown, observed that only 9 labor bills had been passed and that, of these, Del Sesto had vetoed 2. Brown described the session as "very disappointing." [58] He felt that the situation could be improved only if labor participated in both the Democratic and the Republican primaries.

In July the AFL-CIO legislative committee issued its report. It claimed that there was hardly any difference between the political parties, that the Democrats were as reactionary as the Republicans. Although critical of Senator Sgambato, the report praised other Democratic legislative leaders who, however, were "not able to deliver" on their commitments for specific legislation. The report also stated that because the Senate made its decisions behind closed committee doors, it was a difficult body to work with.[59]

Governor Del Sesto was also giving labor difficulties. He appointed three members to his Advisory Council on Employment Security without consulting the AFL-CIO. Two of the three appointees belonged to independent non-AFL-CIO unions.[60] The AFL-CIO protested, and when another council seat became available, Del Sesto offered to make his appointment from a list of five names to be submitted by the state labor organization. The AFL-CIO refused to submit a list.[61]

The AFL-CIO broke precedent in September by refusing to invite either Democratic or Republican politicians to its Labor Day picnic.[62] At the picnic Policastro held out the prospect of peace with the Democrats, on the condition that the party prove itself by passing labor bills.[63] Meanwhile Lieutenant Governor Notte attempted to improve labor–party relations by meeting privately with labor leaders and by publicly praising Policastro and Brown.[64] Sensing a chance to make new political friends, the Republicans, too, were seeking better relations with labor. Del Sesto invited 27 AFL-CIO leaders to a Statehouse breakfast. At the breakfast the Governor and the labor leaders discussed a state fund for workmen's compensation, among other issues, and they agreed upon procedures for future consultations.[65] Speaking before the East Side Republican Club in November, nearly a month after the breakfast, Edwin C. Brown said: "Organized labor in Rhode Island is not tied up with the Democratic party, but supports those whose voting record and activities are favorable to it." [66] Brown also said that labor had reached no judgment on the Del Sesto administration.

As the 1960 legislative session began in January, labor sought good relations with both the Republican Governor and the Assembly Democrats. Ten AFL-CIO leaders met with Del Sesto to ask him to support their program; he in turn asked them to support parts of his program.[67] Four AFL-CIO leaders were hosts at a luncheon for Democratic legislative leaders. The labor leaders asked for no specific promises but rather for guarantees of fair consideration for their bills. They particularly hoped that their proposals would not die in committee.[68]

In this election-year Assembly session, labor was more successful than it had been in the previous session. Thirty-three labor bills were passed, a record. Governor Del Sesto, however, vetoed 9 of them. One, a much-sought-after antistrike-breaker act, he vetoed twice. The AFL-CIO accused him of having an antilabor bias.[69]

As the elections approached, the AFL-CIO involved itself deeply in Democratic party affairs. It endorsed Roberts' comeback bid for the United States Senate seat vacated by Theodore Francis Green. Labor leaders were also reportedly active in clandestine efforts to head off a gubernatorial primary by persuading former Lieutenant Governor Armand Cote not to challenge Lieutenant Governor Notte.[70] Del Sesto referred to these AFL-CIO activists as "frustrated politicians," [71] and the Republican state chairman, in declining an invitation to bring his candidate before the AFL-CIO executive board, made it clear that his party would try to appeal directly to labor's rank and file.[72]

At their Labor Day picnic AFL-CIO leaders urged workers to vote for Democrats.[73] The AFL-CIO was spending over $30,000 in the campaign. Initial efforts were not encouraging, however. Roberts, who had labor's backing, was ignominiously defeated in the primary. A Democratic-party-endorsed nominee for the office of lieutenant governor, Edward P. Gallogly, had been opposed by labor, which had backed the staunchly prolabor former mayor of Pawtucket. Yet Gallogly won easily, obtaining in the process independent endorsement from the Electricians Union and a former state AFL official.[74] On the other hand, John A. Notte, Jr., did win his primary, and sharing labor's blanket endorsement of all of the Democratic candidates for state offices, he went on to win the governorship in the general election.[75] Labor also endorsed 21 Assembly candidates, 20 of whom were Democrats.

After the November election the AFL-CIO held its first state-wide convention. One of the speakers was Vincent J. Sirabella, a former Rhode Island CIO officer whose union had transferred him to Connecticut. Sirabella boasted from the rostrum that in 1956 and again in 1958 labor had saved Governor-elect Notte from "political extinction." Labor, he said, should now call on Notte to "redeem his debt." [76] Some reports had Sirabella claiming, "We own him." Notte, who was vacationing in Florida, wired back a denial: "No one owns me." [77]

During January, 1961, Governor Notte spent much of his time on appointments of interest to labor. The AFL-CIO executive board endorsed Arthur Devine for a post in the administration but was itself divided as to whether Devine should be reappointed Director of Labor.[78] Notte reacted by naming Devine to the lucrative post of State Racing Steward.

Then he appointed an East Providence attorney with a graduate degree in labor law and experience with the National Labor Relations Board to be Director of Labor. Whatever his qualifications, Notte's designee, Clifford J. Cawley, Jr., had no connections with the state AFL-CIO.[79] Next, Notte named the owner of a nonunion printing shop, Albert Fascio, to be the public member of a review board. The appointment of Fascio was an effort to make peace with the Cote wing of the state Democratic party. Labor was upset that it had no influence on this appointment.[80] Despite labor's objections, the Democratic-controlled Senate confirmed Fascio's appointment without even a hearing.

On February 17 the AFL-CIO wrote to its constituent unions, notifying them that a total breakdown in relations with Governor Notte was imminent. Labor's specific grievances were that the Governor had failed to name a labor representative to his new fiscal study commission, that he had appointed Fascio to the review board, that he would not sponsor a people's counsel bill, and that he had refused an invitation to meet with AFL-CIO officials. The AFL-CIO letter was signed by both Policastro and Brown.[81] In response Notte said that he would meet with labor officials as soon as possible.[82]

On February 27 the AFL-CIO announced a "modest program" for the 1961 legislative session. Aside from a higher minimum wage, most of its proposals involved changes in workmen's compensation and unemployment compensation.[83] Labor bills were discussed when, on March 2, Governor Notte held his promised meeting with the AFL-CIO leaders. The meeting lasted three hours and was officially described as "constructive and amiable." [84] Soon thereafter Notte introduced a state income tax proposal. His bill called for fixed rates and a corresponding reduction in the sales tax from 3 to 2 per cent. In the community at large, Notte's plan generated much opposition. The AFL-CIO, long known to favor an income tax, reacted by introducing its own income tax bill, which provided for graduated rates and elimination of the sales tax within three years.[85] Widespread opposition forced Notte to withdraw his bill in a devastating political defeat. Labor, meanwhile, criticized him for not accepting its proposal for the tax.[86]

In May AFL-CIO leaders met with Democratic legislative leaders and members of the House Labor Committee to discuss their proposals. The labor leaders criticized Notte, who was defended by the Democratic politicians.[87] When the session ended, none of the 15 official AFL-CIO bills that had been proposed had been passed. The antistrikebreakers bill and the minimum-wage bill had died in the Senate Labor Committee, whose chairman was now Senator Francis Smith of Woonsocket. Of the 27 bills that had been introduced by the AFL-CIO for its affiliate unions, 6 had passed, as had 2 labor bills sponsored by the Notte administration and 3 labor bills proposed independently by Democratic legislators.[88]

Surveying the results, the AFL-CIO secretary-treasurer, Edwin C. Brown, called the session "disastrous as far as the working people of the state are concerned." Labor, in his view, had "reaped a harvest of broken political promises." [89] The AFL-CIO's annual legislative report said that "a large segment of the Democratic party has been captured by reactionary forces" and that "never in our memory has organized labor received so little from the General Assembly as in 1961." [90]

No politicians were invited to the 1961 Labor Day picnic. President Policastro, of the AFL-CIO, used the occasion to say: "We believe that some of our political leaders have either joined forces with the advocates of the *status quo* or turned their backs on the basic philosophy of the Democratic party." [91] Labor leaders met with Notte one more time before the year ended. The Governor indicated that he would introduce an antistrikebreakers bill himself, and he reviewed some 20 other labor proposals. He called the talks "harmonious and constructive," but Policastro said, "All we did was review his program." [92]

For 1962 labor prepared a more modest legislative program. Among its items were a people's counsel bill, changes in workmen's compensation, collective bargaining for state and municipal employees, an antistrikebreaking bill, and a minimum wage of $1.25 an hour.[93] Representatives of industry were quick to challenge labor's program, and Edwin Brown and the AFL-CIO counsel, Julius Michaelson, met with Governor Notte to discuss the situation.[94] Still, soon after this meeting the labor leaders took an open stand against Notte's decision to legalize night horse racing. Policastro, Brown, and Michaelson appeared before the State Racing Commission to testify against Notte's position. In addition to opposing the administration's stand on racing, labor kept up its efforts to increase state control over the Blue Cross and Physicians Service.[95]

On April 13, at an emotional AFL-CIO executive board meeting, the Democratic party was roundly condemned. Labor endorsed Lawrence Spitz for governor. Calling Rhode Island a "no-party state," those present at the meeting said that the Democratic and the Republican parties were identical. Labor was unhappy with the Notte administration; with the Senate Labor Committee chairman, Francis P. Smith; with the House Labor Committee chairman, Thomas P. McHugh; and also with former Governor Roberts, now counsel for Blue Cross and Physicians Service. Spitz called the legislators "more the friends of the doctors, the breweries, and the race tracks than they are of the laboring man." [96] Brown added: "I cannot conceive how representatives of labor can ask the membership to support the present individuals masquerading as Democrats." [97]

After this meeting the AFL-CIO let it be known that some new courses of action were under consideration. One of its committees was studying the legal procedures involved in forming a third party. The AFL-CIO secretary-treasurer, Edwin C. Brown, implied that labor might do better to support a Republican than a Democrat for governor. He revealed that he and Policastro, the AFL-CIO president, had met with former Governor Del Sesto, and also with John H. Chafee, an announced candidate for the Republican gubernatorial nomination. They were to meet with Chafee's primary opponent, Louis V. Jackvony. Brown said that the labor leaders were exploring the possibility of "coalition with other groups." [98] He also reported that they had met with one declared Democratic gubernatorial aspirant, Mayor Kevin Coleman of Woonsocket, but that no discussions with Governor Notte were scheduled.

The AFL-CIO's legislative report, which was published at the end of the session, asserted that both parties had been captured by "reactionary elements." The Democrats were described as placing "the interests of race tracks, insurance companies, medical lobbies, liquor dealers, and self-seeking political hacks ahead of the welfare of the general public." [99] Notte was alleged to be trying to divide the labor movement by distributing appointments and other favors to members of organized labor.

These assertions evoked varying responses. The Electricians Union broke with the AFL-CIO; its president, Thomas F. Kearney, called a third-party movement "suicide" and defended Notte and the Democratic party. The Democratic state chairman, John G. McWeeney, claimed that by the yardstick of legislation benefiting workers, labor had been well treated during the Assembly session. Former Governor Del Sesto found the labor leaders' realization that the Democrats had used them as "pawns" to be "refreshing," and he counseled against a third party. [100] The Republican state chairman, William T. Broomhead, was pleased that the AFL-CIO had joined with him "in recognizing that the Democratic party is not the party of the working man." [101] Finally, the Director of Labor, Clifford J. Cawley, Jr., who was a Democrat, spoke out for Notte and his record; he said that the Governor was a "liberal." [102]

Throughout the summer the AFL-CIO grappled with the problem of what to do about the oncoming elections. Notte was severely challenged in a primary by Mayor Coleman of Woonsocket, himself a former Machinists Union business agent. But since Coleman and Senator Smith were allies, labor made no primary endorsements. Then the AFL-CIO executive board decided to stick to a nonendorsement policy for the general election as well. The internal consensus for this decision was "overwhelming." [103] No politicians were invited to the Labor Day picnic, and the AFL-CIO declined the requests of both parties to submit labor planks to their respective platform committees.[104]

As the election approached without labor endorsements or activity, the Democratic state chairman, John G. McWeeney, said that he counted upon workers to support the party as they had in the past. Individual unions, such as the Electricians and the Laborers, endorsed the party slate.[105] On October 12, the AFL-CIO endorsed the Democratic Congressional candidates, 21 Democrats running for the Assembly, and a single Republican Assembly contender. There was no endorsement of general state officers. The *Providence Journal* reported that at a last-minute executive board meeting on October 31, labor had offered the Democratic party leaders an endorsement of all state candidates except Notte, a proposal that was declined.[106] Thus, Notte became the first Democrat since the 1930's to run without official support from labor. Further, on November 1, the AFL-CIO secretary-treasurer, Edwin C. Brown, called a proposal made by Notte's opponent, John H. Chafee, to take along a labor official on a nine-state search for new industries, "a novel and excellent idea." [107]

The 1962 gubernatorial election, like that of 1956, was not

decided until the absentee ballots were counted. While the count was proceeding, labor leaders were asked how they felt about Notte's situation. Brown was noncommittal about Notte, but he expressed delight that all of the candidates whom labor had supported had won. He added: "We did not try to hurt Notte. We just did not go out to help him." Brown revealed that labor had saved a great deal of money during the campaign, money that usually went for workers and advertising. He also suggested that labor's inactivity might have affected Notte's poor showing in Pawtucket, a strong labor community in which there had been a very light turnout of voters. Asked how he thought labor would do with a Republican in the Statehouse and the same Democratic-controlled legislature as before, Brown said: "I think we'll have better success up there because we can't have any worse than we had." [108]

III / THE LABOR EXECUTIVE
BOARD MEMBERS

Labor executive board members in Rhode Island were local union leaders who represented their international or local organizations on the governing boards of the AFL, the CIO, or the AFL-CIO between 1952 and 1962.[1] Within labor their responsibilities were seen as twofold: they had to convey worker sentiment to the state labor organizations, and they had to carry back messages from the state organizations to the grass roots. The latter responsibility was especially heavy, since state labor organizations never attempted direct communication by mail with workers. If state policies were to be translated into local action, the crucial individuals would be the executive board members. The attitudes of the executive board members would thus affect decisions made by the state organizations and the success with which those decisions would be carried out. Labor executive board members could be described as the middle-level management in the labor organizations and in labor–political-party relations. For the purposes of this book, the executive board members' perceptions of, and attitudes toward, the Democratic party in Rhode Island should be revealing as to the past course and future direction of the labor–party relationship.

A Profile of the Labor Executive Board Members

Although there was a great difference in age between national AFL and CIO leaders, this was not the case in Rhode Island; the executive board members of both state organizations were relatively young, forty-seven in 1957, the mid-point of the 1952–62 period.[2] The Rhode Island labor executive board members showed a common educational background: local union leaders were a high-school-educated group and had a higher level of education than the general population of the state.

Not surprisingly, the executive board members from AFL unions had been in the trade-union movement longer than those from CIO unions, since there were no firmly organized CIO shops until the late 1930's. But all of the executive board members who were interviewed had entered the labor movement by 1950. All of them demonstrated a uniform career pattern. Of the 25 interviewed, 17 were full-time union officials, 6 were part-time officials, and 2 had other occupations. None were full-time workers whose only income came from their trades. Some served as business agents, local officers, or international representatives to a cluster of locals. Whatever their titles, however, the work they did was similar. They were the bureaucrats of the labor movement, the "walking delegates" of and to the local units; they were close to the concrete, day-to-day problems of the unions.

There were some ethnic differences between the AFL and the CIO executive board members and between the executive board members generally and the Rhode Island population. The CIO board members were more likely to be of Italo-American origin than were those of the AFL. One board member observed: "The AFL was all Irish and English. The CIO had the Italians and all of the 'out' groups." Of the board member population taken together, however, 11 of 25 were of Irish origin; this proportion was twice as large as that in the Rhode Island total population. Apparently the Rhode Island unions, like the state political parties, were vehicles for upwardly mobile members of minority immigrant groups.

The Political Activity of Rhode Island Unions

It seemed reasonable to consider the labor executive board members good sources of information about the pattern of political activity among Rhode Island labor unions. When interviewed, most of the board members tended to talk about the activities of their international union in the state, rather than their particular local union unit; the scope of the resulting data is, therefore, broader than the local unit but still narrower than the over-all AFL, CIO, or AFL-CIO. For example, answers refer to the Rubber Workers Union, rather than to Local 6 or to the state CIO.

The first question on Table 1 shows a significantly different level of perception among the local leaders as to the degrees of political activity engaged in by the members of their unions. If the perceptions are accurate, and one may assume that they are, then CIO members were much more inclined to participate in state politics as individuals than were AFL members. Taking the total for the two organizations, 64 per cent of the board members came from unions whose members participated in politics to some degree. The same pattern of greater CIO participation occurred at the level of union activity, as the second question on Table 1 indicates. All of the CIO leaders said that their unions were involved in politics, while slightly less than half of the AFL leaders said that theirs were involved—a statistically significant difference in levels of activity. As an average, 68 per cent of the board members belonged to unions that participated in politics to some degree.

TABLE 1

LABOR'S PARTICIPATION IN RHODE ISLAND POLITICS

QUESTION/ANSWER	NUMBER OF RESPONDENTS		
	AFL (15)	CIO (10)	Total (25)
1. Do the members of your union participate in state politics as individuals?[a]			
Yes	7	9	16
No	8	1	9
2. Did your union itself participate in state politics between 1952 and 1962?[b]			
Yes	7	10	17
No	8	0	8
3. Which of the following forms of political activity did your union engage in?			
Providing funds	4	8	12
Providing workers	6	9	15
Providing endorsements	7	10	17
Encouraging members to seek office	8	8	16
4. Did the members of your union live concentrated in particular election districts?			
Yes	2	4	6
No	13	6	19

[a]The difference between AFL and CIO "Yes" responses is statistically significant at the .05 level on the Fisher Exact Probability Test.
[b]The difference between AFL and CIO "Yes" responses is statistically significant at the .01 level on the Fisher Exact Probability Test.

Unions can contribute to political campaigns in several ways. They can provide funds or workers for candidates, they can endorse candidates and thus influence the votes of their members, and they can encourage their members to seek office.

For candidates for office, funds and workers were probably labor's most valuable tangible contributions, followed closely by endorsement. The third question on Table 1 shows the ways in which the AFL and the CIO locals participated in Rhode Island politics. The CIO pattern of participation was high throughout all of the possible categories of involvement, whereas the AFL unions contributed in an inverse order of maximum utility to the politicians, being most inclined to encourage their own men to run and least inclined to give funds to candidates. In general, contributions were the least popular form of union participation. Further, about half of the Rhode Island unions provided some funds, over half provided workers, close to two-thirds encouraged their members to seek office, and over two-thirds endorsed candidates.There are no studies to compare with this data for Rhode Island, but if the perceptions of the executive board members are correct, one would have to conclude that individual unions participated widely in state politics between 1952 and 1962.

Union endorsement, more than any other type of political activity, depends on how well the union communicates its decisions to its members, how the members are dispersed geographically, and whether the workers will follow their leaders' advice. It is difficult to explain exactly how decisions to endorse were conveyed to union members because only 4 of 10 CIO board members and 2 of 15 AFL board members could recall their unions' using a newsletter to communicate with workers during the 1952–62 period. Of course decisions could always have been transmitted orally. Further, if endorsements were for state representatives or senators who came from compact districts, there must have been distinct limits to how much help the unions could offer. As the fourth question on Table 1 indicates, only 2 of 15 AFL board members and 4 of 10 CIO board members perceived that their unions' workers lived in compact areas and therefore were able to make their weight felt at the polls. Still, those few who did perceive this fact realized that their members were concentrated in areas in a number of cities. Union districts, according to the board members' accounts, existed in Cranston, Providence, Warwick, Pawtucket, Bristol, Woonsocket, and West Warwick. Whether workers acted on leadership endorsement is a question that will be considered later in this book.

The tabular data do not measure the content or intensity of union participation in politics. Selected comments, however, may convey the flavor of the board members' replies when they were interviewed. From the AFL, an Electricians Union officer observed that his members participated "quite a lot" as individuals. Noting that two of his members were Democratic representatives at one time, a Machinists Union official said that there was great union concentration in Woonsocket: "All of our real successful activists are from there." A Garment Workers Union representative commented: "About 40 per cent of our membership lives in Pawtucket. But that hasn't given us any special influence in Pawtucket politics." And a Painters Union leader explained that the officers were the activists: "It's hard to get members interested," he said.

From the CIO, a Brewery Workers Union leader said enthusiastically: "We have had members elected as councilmen in Cranston and Providence. Many of our people are on ward committees." A prevalent CIO attitude was revealed by an Insurance Workers Union officer: "Our members have been representatives from Pawtucket and Providence. You can lose everything you win at the negotiating table at the Statehouse." A Steelworkers Union official believed that members of his union were inclined to participate "in greater proportion than in other organizations," while an official of the Textile Workers Union of America considered participation "an economic necessity for textiles."

Since the labor executive board members participated on both the decision-making and operational levels of the state AFL, CIO, and AFL-CIO, their perceptions of the scope of the political activities of the Rhode Island labor organizations should be accurate and revealing. All of the executive board members agreed that the state labor organizations were involved in politics in Rhode Island between 1952 and 1962. They were unanimous in feeling that this involvement included efforts in general elections and in the legislature; however, only 11 of the 25 board members who were interviewed could recall participation by their state organizations in primaries. Yet the public record suggested that state labor organizations were sometimes quite heavily involved in primaries. The lack of perception of primary activity could signal either internal disagreement about the propriety of involvement in primaries or a backward projection of present disapproval of this type of participation.

Over two-thirds of the labor executive board members recalled that the state organizations had contributed funds to candidates or parties between 1952 and 1962, with the proviso that in most cases contributions were "relatively small" amounts. It was stressed that these funds were returns from the national AFL-CIO Committee on Political Education (COPE) and went to labor-endorsed candidates. All of the board members agreed that the state organizations had provided workers for candidates. There was also consensus on the ways in which the workers were made available and were directed. As a rule, the workers were assigned to voter registration during the campaign; on election day they took people to the polls and checked voting lists. Almost always the workers were directed by union officials. Labor endorsements and reports on campaign activities were communicated by the state organization to local union leaders, two-thirds of the board members recalled, primarily by means of a newsletter. The newsletter went only to officials, yet one-third of the board members could not remember ever having received it. Several board members also mentioned that on occasion labor had placed paid advertisements in the *Providence Journal* to endorse candidates.

Once again, selected comments can convey some of the tone of the board members' responses to questions about the state labor organizations. From the AFL half of the AFL-CIO, a leader said: "When we contributed, we gave relatively small amounts. It was all refunds to the state from COPE. COPE is sure the Rhode Island Congressional candidates are secure, so it would rather spend money in problem areas." Another official explained: "We contributed through COPE a fair share. Our people worked on registration, worked closely with the AFL-CIO. Sometimes locals sent workers directly to candidates." Another said that the pattern was irregular: "Primarily, we did registration, telephoning, getting out the vote. Sometimes it was co-ordinated from the AFL-CIO office and sometimes just done through locals. It was all volunteer work."

From the CIO half of the alliance, one leader observed that for the state organizations, "workers were our greatest contribution. They were under union direction and worked with union people." Another was not as enthusiastic about the role of the unions: "The locals provided the workers, all on a voluntary basis. We were really dependent upon individuals." And a third leader recalled: "We contributed a lot of work but were never in a position to give much money. We had girls, working on registration, and drivers consistently over the ten-year period." Still another explained: "We contributed the returns from COPE, perhaps an average of $2,000–$4,000 per year. We contributed either to the party chairman or to candidates when we were the CIO; the merged AFL-CIO has stayed away from the party and gone straight to the candidates." Finally, one officer remembered that the CIO in its early stage "really had workers, especially for Roberts and the general officers. Unions, the CIO, were on the upswing then."

The Labor Executive Board Members' Perceptions of Labor and the Democratic Party

There are two considerations in the labor executive board members' perceptions of the labor–party relationship: first, how they viewed the efforts made by labor on behalf of the Democratic party; and second, how they evaluated what labor received from the party in return. Of the 25 executive board members interviewed, 6 felt that state labor organization endorsements were "very important" to candidates and 13 felt that the endorsements were "important." Thus, a very high value was placed upon endorsements by those who did the endorsing. Further, it was agreed that endorsement was a useful activity. Three board members said that endorsements were "very important" because they affected labor's postelection influence and 15 called the endorsements "important" for the same reason. Two members said that endorsements had been important after elections only until 1958, that after then they were of no help.

In evaluating their organizations in terms of over-all political activities, 8 labor executive board members said that labor was "very effective," while 15 said that it was "effective." Five thought that labor's efforts to obtain legislation were "very effective" and 13 thought that labor's lobbyists were "effective." A strong minority of 7 said that after 1958 labor was "ineffective" in obtaining legislation. However, all 25 board members felt that the state AFL-CIO was "consulted" by Democratic governors and legislators at least "sometimes." (Eleven of the 25 said that the labor organizations were consulted "often.") It was stressed that the consultations were generally limited to matters concerning labor.

The image that the labor executive board members had of their own groups' participation in politics was decidedly positive. From the AFL half of the AFL-CIO alliance, a leader described labor endorsements as "important to a lot of politicians." Another official believed that "the labor vote is very helpful and brings in other votes." A third board member said that "endorsements are very important if they are done in the right way." Still a fourth leader stated: "Sympathetic candidates expect our support, and it's only fair." From the

CIO half of the alliance, a leader affirmed that endorsements led to results in the legislature. "We got people appointed to committees and chairmanships. We had success on party platforms." An experienced official remarked: "You can't expect anything if you don't help those who are sympathetic to you." A third official commented: "It was a good thing we committed ourselves—it helps us in getting our program enacted in the Assembly." But another board member remembered: "We have had unfortunate experiences. We have endorsed, worked for a candidate, then got ignored."

All of the respondents agreed that they had had easy access. "I never had any trouble seeing the Governor when I went up there on union business," said one leader. Another observed that "consultations were regular with all administrations —Del Sesto and Notte, too." And a third officer explained: "They didn't always agree with us, but they would always talk." Speaking of legislative rewards, one official confided: "We didn't do bad except under Notte." Another board member elaborated: "The key was the close relationship between Roberts and the leaders of labor. They worked together on the legislature." But one official said: "We had to fight like hell for a few pieces every now and then." Or, in the words of a different board member: "We got fair consideration, although we didn't always get what we wanted." Finally, another leader said: "When labor went up there, we were treated with less consideration than other lobbies—business, insurance, etc., particularly since the Landrum-Griffin Bill passed."

The labor executive board members were considerably less affirmative in their attitudes toward labor's relations with the Democratic party. The first question on Table 2 contains data that seem to agree with the public record given in Chapter I. Up to 1958 almost all of the respondents felt that the labor–party relationship was at least "satisfactory," and a good proportion even felt that it was "very satisfactory." Yet 15 board members then added, in effect: "But after 1958, the relation-

TABLE 2

QUESTION/ANSWER	NUMBER OF RESPONDENTS		
	AFL (15)	CIO (10)	Total (25)
1. Would you describe the relationship between the state AFL-CIO and the Democratic party in Rhode Island as:			
Very satisfactory	3	0	3
Satisfactory	4	2	6
Unsatisfactory	0	1	1
Very satisfactory to 1958, unsatisfactory thereafter	3	7	10
Satisfactory to 1958, unsatisfactory thereafter	5	0	5
2. Within your memory, has labor's influence within the Democratic party changed?			
Yes	6	5	11
No	7	2	9
Don't know/won't answer	2	3	5
3. Would you say that labor was *more* influential in the Democratic party in the 1930's and the 1940's than in the 1950's?			
Yes	2	4	6
No—no difference	2	2	4
No—less influential in the earlier period	1	1	2
No—most influential in the 1940's and 1950's	2	1	3
Don't know/won't answer	8	2	10
4. Would you say that labor was *more* influential in the Democratic party in the 1950's than in the early 1960's?			
Yes	9	8	17
No—no difference	4	1	5
No—less influential in the earlier period	0	0	0
Don't know/won't answer	2	1	3

ship became unsatisfactory from our point of view." Thus, taking into account the single board member who felt that things were always bad, 16 of 25, or 64 per cent, evaluated the relationship as poor after 1958. The shift in sentiment was especially marked among the CIO respondents.

The second question on Table 2 contains data that approach the labor–party relationship in another way. The board members were asked: "Within your memory, has labor's influence within the Democratic party changed?" Over half of the respondents—11 of 20—said that it had. Then, to determine the direction of the change, the executive board members were asked if they thought that labor was more influential in the Democratic party during the 1930's and the 1940's than during the 1950's. The response was mainly in the negative, as the third question on Table 2 indicates. One would have to conclude that the board members had no clear perceptions, as a group, of the direction of any change between the 1930's and the 1950's in the Rhode Island labor–party coalition. When the focus was shifted, however, to the difference between the 1950's and the 1960's, a very clear perception emerged.

Of 22 respondents, 17 answered affirmatively to the fourth question on Table 2: "Would you say that labor was more influential in the Democratic party in the 1950's than in the early 1960's?" This response clearly pinpoints the time and the direction of the perceived change.[3]

Selected comments illustrate the attitudes with which the labor executive board members viewed the Democratic party's treatment of labor. Five AFL board members made the following statements:

> The relationship was very satisfactory to us under Roberts. We were very close to him and got great legislation under him. Notte was an inconsistent personality—tried to be friendly to everyone. The times may have been right for passing labor legislation during the 1930's, 1940's, and 1950's. There was a change

with the Eisenhower years—its policy filtered down—through the NLRB, for example.

Roberts pretty much controlled the party in the House and Senate. Roberts could deliver leaders and members of the legislature. The difficulty with Notte was lack of leadership on his part. The Democratic party scattered all over the place. The Democrats thought they had us in their back pocket and told us so. That's when *we* started to get a little apart.

The split was a matter of personalities. But you'll never see labor as strong as it was in the past. Times have changed. There's a new breed of labor leaders today, and a new breed in the Democratic party, too.

The change was in the labor group—after the merger. No change in the Democrats—labor wanted results.

We just seemed to have a closer relationship during the 1950's —partially a matter of personalities.

Four CIO board members made these remarks:

Roberts was the best governor the state ever had. Notte was just a figurehead; he figured he had us in his hip pocket and he ignored us, ignored the people who worked for him and gave him the opportunity to be governor. I disagree with those in labor who say labor is most effective politically as a free agent.

We were not as effective after 1958. I don't really think labor has changed. It is the people in the party—they seem to show more resentment in the lobbying and bury our bills in committee. A matter of personalities—new faces in the Democratic party.

We have less influence than we had a few years ago. Our biggest influence was the Speaker of the House, Harry Curvin. The CIO saved him from defeat in the early 1950's. Curvin was always a good friend of labor; he had more influence getting our program through than anyone but Roberts, and after 1954 we were more successful with him than we were with Roberts.

At one time, all the labor policymakers were on the state payroll—our inner group. We got a lot out of this relationship, but became tools of the party after a while. The best thing Brown, Spitz, and Policastro have done is end this political job business.

The basic source of change is our workers. People are no longer voting the straight party. Something has happened.

Conclusions

From the data in this chapter a number of conclusions can be drawn about labor–Democratic-party relations in Rhode Island. The labor executive board members reported that their own unions participated in politics to a considerable degree, with endorsement of candidates the most popular means of supporting the party. They also saw the state AFL, CIO, and AFL-CIO as involved in Rhode Island politics and as effective in making real contributions to the Democratic party. Further, in keeping with this positive image of labor's role in the labor–party relationship, the board members perceived labor as being successful in sponsoring and obtaining legislation favorable to it.

Yet, in a manner that signals an uncertain future for labor–party relations, the labor executive board members did not view the Democratic party as positively as they viewed their own groups. From 1958 on, they perceived labor–party relations as unsatisfactory; they perceived a decline in labor's influence within the Democratic party from the 1950's to the 1960's. Their perceptions of a decline seem to constitute evidence for the hypothesis of this book, that the old labor–party coalition was coming apart and that labor was beginning to feel itself able to operate as a free agent and to improve its situation. In Chapter I it was suggested that the Democratic party, while not rejecting labor's support, would feel that it could achieve its goals independently of the alliance with labor that was once its byword. The perceptions of the Democrats will be examined in the next chapter.

IV / THE LEGISLATORS

Labor organizations in Rhode Island often brought legislative proposals to the Rhode Island General Assembly. The Democrats controlled the House of Representatives through 1958, and from then until 1962 they controlled both branches of the state legislature. This chapter is concerned with labor–party relations in the Assembly as they were reflected in the behavior and perceptions of the legislators of the Democratic party.

State Legislatures and State Legislators

State legislatures are bound by legal and party ties to the governor and the judiciary. At the same time, through party connections, interest-group activity, and the influence of public opinion, they are brought into association with groups outside the statehouse. Yet legislatures demonstrate some of the behavioral characteristics of the closed group. They have patterns of behavior, developed over a period of time, to which new members are expected to conform. Also they have formal and informal rules that are designed to facilitate the working out of problems by men who may disagree on general outlook and on specific details; the rules make it possible for members to disagree without becoming disagreeable.[1]

The state legislator, unlike his federal counterpart, is often a part-time politician whose main source of income is his private occupation. Usually his occupation allows time for politics, and it may even be furthered by political activity.[2] In most states the legislator cannot support himself on his legislative salary alone—in Rhode Island, for example, it was limited to $300 a year by the state constitution. One way for him to overcome this limitation is to "use his position to obtain other rewards, either directly through political action or through the aid that political action gives him in another occupation." [3] In most state legislatures one finds a high proportion of lawyers, small businessmen, and insurance and real-estate salesmen. This was certainly the case in the Rhode Island General Assembly for the 1952–62 period. In 1956 in the House of Representatives the Democrats had the following occupational distribution: 25 per cent were lawyers or members of other professions; 32 per cent were self-employed small businessmen; 27 per cent were sales personnel; 13 per cent were either labor officials or manual workers; and the rest were retired persons. None was in a managerial position.

The occupational spread also reflects another characteristic of the Rhode Island state legislator. He usually came from a lower-middle-class background, and especially in the Democratic party, he was likely to belong to one of several minority ethnic groups that utilized politics as a vehicle for upward mobility. When the ethnic origins of all of the Democratic legislators who served in the Assembly from 1932 through 1962 were analyzed, 41 per cent were found to be Irish. This figure corroborates the view of other observers that for some time the Irish had been dominant within the Democratic party. Further, 21 per cent of the legislators were French, and 17 per cent were Italian. The rise of the Italo-Americans within the Democratic party ranks in the Assembly was noticeable in the 1952–62 period.

Finally, like the participants in any institution, the state legislator has a role. John C. Wahlke and his co-authors maintained that the concept of role provided the best explanation for a legislator's behavior in many areas, including his relation to interest groups.[4] A role was defined by Wahlke and his associates as a status, a set of mutual expectations about behavior possessed by all the participants. A legislator possesses a set of expectations about his own role, which was found by the Wahlke investigators to be distinctive. The legislator also possesses perceptions about the proper role of an interest group. What he perceives as legitimate interest-group activity as well as what he perceives as the "supposedly objective 'facts' of such activity" are related to his own role.[5] Along with a general legislative role that affects the behavior of the state legislator, Wahlke found a more specialized leader role, a set of expectations about the proper activity of the party leader.

The Characteristics and Recruitment of the Legislators in the Rhode Island General Assembly

Three categories of legislators in the Rhode Island General Assembly—labor legislators, Democratic legislators, and Democratic legislative leaders—have already been established in Chapter I. When labor legislators and rank-and-file Democratic legislators are referred to, the term "ordinary legislators" will be used, to differentiate them from the Democratic legislative leaders. The legislators were interviewed so that information could be obtained about the relationship of labor and the Democratic party in Rhode Island, and some propositions about interest-group–party relations could be tested. For these purposes the labor legislators formed an apt population for study. If a range of activists in the interest-group–party relationship were visualized, the labor legislators would occupy the mid-point between the labor executive board members, who were involved almost exclusively in the affairs of labor, and the political executives, who were politically oriented.

Thus, in Rhode Island labor–party relations could be viewed from the perspective of their effects on the labor legislators.

The phenomenon of labor-associated personnel in American politics has been noted by Professor Harry M. Scoble who said that "the most fundamental postwar change in the structure and process of political parties has been the entrance of organized labor into electoral activity at the precinct level and up." [6] In 1954 a study by a special committee of the American Political Science Association showed Rhode Island to have a larger number of union members in its legislature than any other state, but this study, unfortunately, yielded little of theoretical utility.[7] Likewise, a report by L. G. Seligman on politics in Oregon served only to call attention to the co-ordinate rise of organized labor and the Democratic party in that state.[8] The presence of such scattered and unconnected data led Scoble to ask: "Who in the political science profession is carrying out trend analyses to find out whether, regardless of labor propaganda, labor ideology is in fact being advanced by increasing union representation in state legislatures?" [9] This chapter is intended to shed some light on the general question of labor representation in state legislatures as well as on the behavior of different categories of legislators in the Rhode Island General Assembly.

The Democratic legislators and the Democratic legislative leaders in Rhode Island were like their counterparts in other states; they tended to belong to upwardly mobile minority ethnic groups, and they were predominantly self-employed small-businessmen, although a considerable and increasing number of them were lawyers. All of the legislators in the Rhode Island General Assembly had more formal education than the general population of the state, but the Democratic legislative leaders had the most education—70 per cent of them had attended college.

Writers on the subject of state legislative behavior have noted two patterns for the recruitment of legislators: either the legislators were encouraged to enter politics by acquaintances or interest-group members, or else they came from highly political family backgrounds. Heinz Eulau and his associates observed that "state legislators tend to come from families which are much more involved in politics than the average American family." [10] Similarly, in a study of the first-term Connecticut legislators whose futures seemed to be bright, James D. Barber also stressed the importance of family experiences:

At the time of his nomination, the typical Lawmaker could find in his personal background precedents for political action, particularly the precedent of family participation. While there is little evidence on this point, it seems likely that a positive attitude toward taking part in politics seems to be inherited, like party identification. Put another way, Lawmakers need not rely entirely on their interest in issues to move them into politics. Such participation seems natural and legitimate to one raised in a home where politics was not only a topic for discussion but also a matter for action. [11]

Both types of recruitment were found in Rhode Island. However, the Democratic legislators were usually persuaded to enter politics by friends and associates. Fifty-three per cent of the Democratic legislators ran for office because they had been asked to, even though most of them had had no previous political experience at the time. Twenty per cent said that family background had been the major influence on their decisions to enter politics. The rest became politicians because of personal interests that had been developed in school, law practice, or business.

The labor legislators might have been expected to have been influenced by labor to enter politics, but less than one fourth of them said that labor had had any effect on their becoming candidates. They were recruited in the same ways as the Democratic legislators. The ways in which the latter were brought into politics are revealed in their comments:

Three or four fellows in the neighborhood asked me if I would be a candidate—this was my first interest in politics. I became interested about the time I became a candidate.

I was asked to run. I never had any ambitions. I was suggested to the District Committee. They picked me because I was Jewish, had a big family, and could win.

I picked up the political bug from my father's interest in ward politics.

My law career was important—law school whetted my interest.

The Democratic legislative leaders, in contrast, almost always entered politics because of their family backgrounds. Five of the seven leaders who were interviewed came from families that had a strong interest in politics. The leaders recalled:

I was brought up in a political family. My father ran for public office, but the property qualification kept him down. I was more successful than he was.

My father took an active interest in politics as a younger man. He was later a statehouse and city hall reporter for the *Providence Journal*. It was something I grew up with.

I was brought up in politics. My father was in it and I just drifted into it. He was an alderman and I used to go around with him.

The Legislators' Relations with Labor in Rhode Island

Relations between labor and the legislators in the Rhode Island General Assembly were based on campaign aid and legislative support. Campaign aid consisted of funds, workers, and endorsement of candidates, and was given by labor to the legislators. Legislative support was given by the legislators to labor, and it involved proposing labor bills; working for such bills on the floor, in committees, and in party caucuses; and voting for them. One of the objects of this study was to find out what the relations were between each type of legislator and labor. Who did what for whom? Were there differences in the extent of campaign aid and legislative support that the different categories of legislators received?

Campaign aid for legislators in Rhode Island did not have the overriding urgency that it had in other states because, during the 1952–62 period, the turnover of seats in the General Assembly was small. Only 22 of the 144 Senate and House districts underwent party changes. What shifting there was took place in the direction of increased Democratic control. The Democratic margin in the House increased steadily; the party captured the Senate in 1958 and controlled it from then on. Still, for individual legislators campaign aid could be very helpful. If a legislator perceives his seat as insecure, it does not matter a great deal whether it really is or not. The way in which he sees his situation is what counts.

Labor's potential for helping in campaigns depended in part on the composition of the legislator's district. When asked to identify their districts as working class, middle class, upper class, or mixed, the labor legislators, the Democratic legislators, and the Democratic legislative leaders all gave virtually identical responses. They all said that between 40 and 50 per cent of their constituents were working-class people. Further, all of them agreed that there was a medium-to-high percentage of union members in their constituencies. Thus, under some circumstances, labor could be of considerable assistance in campaigns.

For labor legislators the primary form of support in campaigns was endorsement. Over 60 per cent received this type of help from both their local unions and the state AFL-CIO, while only one third received funds, which came from the state labor organization. Between 40 and 50 per cent of the Democratic legislative leaders and of the Democratic legislators reported that they had also received support from organized labor, and most of them said that money was not involved. It was clear from these interviews that wherever there was help from labor, the prevailing type of support was endorsement. Another kind of support, the help of workers, was given to a speaker of the Rhode Island House of Representatives, an exceptionally powerful figure in the Democratic party between 1952 and 1962, who lived in a closely contested district.

Thus, in Rhode Island labor's relations with the Democratic candidates for the state legislature varied. One can conclude that, not surprisingly in an industrialized state with a large working class, the candidates came from working-class constituencies and received aid from labor primarily in the form of endorsement but also in the forms of funds and workers. Does this mean that labor support in campaigns was greater or less in Rhode Island than in other states? The absence of comparative figures makes it impossible to say.

Labor–party relations in the Rhode Island legislature are best understood through an examination of the labor legislators. Hypothetically, the relationship of the labor legislators with the Democratic party could be exceedingly important for labor because the group-associated legislators have an unusually direct entree. Therefore, the first concern in a study of labor legislators in Rhode Island is the relationship between the number of labor legislators in the General Assembly and the number of labor bills passed. In the period from 1934 to 1962 the number of labor legislators serving in any one session of the Assembly ranged from 10 in 1936 to 25 in 1950. Between 1952 and 1962 there were approximately 16 labor legislators in each session. The number of labor-related bills, as listed in *Rhode Island General Laws,* ranged from 5 in the 1937/38 session to 45 during the 1955/56 session,[12] with no significant correlation between the number of labor legislators and the amount of labor legislation passed.[13]

Yet there were numerous ways in which the labor legislators could help labor. Some of them were revealed by inquiries about the interactions of labor legislators and labor-union officials, and of the actions of the labor legislators in the Assembly. An unclear picture emerged. The 15 labor legislators interviewed indicated that they had maintained different kinds of communications with labor executive board members. Six said that they had conversed frequently with labor officials;

6 said that they were in touch occasionally; and 3 said that they had never talked with anyone from labor. Seven reported that they had worked on Assembly committees to advance labor's interests, and 7 said that they had spoken for labor in Democratic party caucuses. Three said that they had talked informally with colleagues on labor's behalf, and 3 recalled giving prolabor speeches. Thus the data indicate that in the Rhode Island General Assembly organized labor could count on the help, in differing degrees, of about half of its representatives.

The most important single service performed for organized labor by the labor legislators became evident only in interviews with the Democratic legislators. The Democratic legislators perceived themselves as backing labor, as giving labor measures strong voting support. Further, they said that the labor legislators were their source of information about labor bills. They ranked their labor colleagues far ahead of both labor officials outside of the Assembly and Democratic legislative leaders as sources of information. The Democratic legislative leaders, in contrast, ranked labor officials outside of the Assembly first and labor legislators second as sources of information. They were accustomed to dealing with individuals whose positions were at their own level. The Democratic legislative leaders, who managed a very cohesive party in the legislature between 1952 and 1962, customarily used the party caucus to reveal which labor bills would have the support of the party. But they often waited until the last legislative day of the term to make known their decisions. During most of the session, routine communications on labor's program came to the rank-and-file Democratic legislators primarily from the labor legislators.

The Roles and Perceptions of the Legislators and the Labor Leaders in Rhode Island

The hypothesis of this book, that relations between the Democratic party and organized labor in Rhode Island changed fundamentally during the period from 1952 to 1962, has already been stated in Chapter I. Interviews with the labor legislators, Democratic legislators, and Democratic legislative leaders were useful in testing this hypothesis, especially when the legislators' responses were compared with replies from the labor executive board members. The legislators, all Democrats, would be expected to perceive their relations with labor as at least adequate, if not entirely satisfactory, perhaps with different perceptions among the three categories. But the labor respondents would be expected to be very conscious of a change in labor–party relations and to be less satisfied with the relationship. Usually, when an alliance is viewed with satisfaction by one side and with discontent by the other, the relationship faces an uncertain future.

This problem was approached through an analysis of the ways in which the legislators and the labor executive board members perceived different aspects of their relationship. Since people act on what they perceive, it is their perceptions that count. At the same time, there was a problem inherent in pursuing this kind of analysis because the labor legislators belonged to both labor and the Democratic party. Thus it was necessary first to determine whether a given legislator perceived events and relationships from the viewpoint of a labor representative, from that of a party member, or from some other viewpoint. In pursuing this line of inquiry, writers on legislative behavior have provided some information but have also left gaps. In *The Legislative System* Wahlke and his collaborators were forced to conclude that their "data provide only inferential evidence that the legislative role tends to take precedence over the interest-group-member role in cases of conflict." [14]

If the authors of *The Legislative System* were correct in arguing that interest-group affiliation is overridden by the legislative role, then the labor legislators in the Rhode Island General Assembly should have had the same perceptions as the Democratic legislators when the Democratic legislators differed from the labor executive board members. But if Wahlke and his co-authors were incorrect, there were several other possibilities. The labor legislators could have had perceptions that were different from those of the other two groups, and the difference could suggest that dual labor–party membership produced distinctive perceptions in a legislator. Or, the labor legislators could have been like the labor executive board members but unlike their Assembly colleagues in their perception of political events; this discrepancy would suggest that interest-group affiliation could override the legislative role. Or, the labor legislators could have been more like the Democratic legislators than the labor executive board members in their perceptions. Perhaps, then, one could talk of an influential but not of a dominant legislative role for the representatives of labor in the Assembly. All of these possibilities emerged from interviews with the legislators and the labor executive board members.

The interview data are consistent with Wahlke's theory of a predominant legislative role. The labor legislators responded like the Democratic legislators to a number of perceptual questions; however, in another series of questions that compared both sets of legislators with the labor executive board members, there are measurable differences. At the same time, the data also support the hypothesis of this book. The labor executive board members and the labor and Democratic legislators differed in their perception of political events as well as in their assessment of the labor–party relationship.

No statistical difference can be found between the Democratic legislators and the labor legislators in the distribution of their responses to a question that was designed to measure self-perception of behavior in a situation of labor–party conflict. The first question on Table 3 shows that in both sets of legislators approximately the same number of members could recall instances of such disagreement. In both sets the

TABLE 3

Activists' Perceptions of Labor–Party Relations in Rhode Island

PERCEPTION/ASSESSMENT	NUMBER OF RESPONDENTS		
	Democratic Legislators 15	Labor Legislators 15	Labor Executive Board Members, 25
1. How they perceived their own actions in situations of labor–party conflict:			
Sided with labor	2	1	
Sided with party	6	5	
Don't remember any cases	5	5	
Other response	2	4	
2. Assessments of labor's current (1964/65) position in Rhode Island politics: [a]			
a) Is labor as powerful as ever?			
Yes	9	7	
No	4	5	
No answer	2	3	
b) Is labor as important to the Democratic party?			
Yes	8	7	
Yes, with reservations	4	4	
No	3	4	
No answer	0	0	
3. Assessments of labor's overall political activities between 1952 and 1962: [b]			
Very effective	4	2	8
Effective	5	6	15
Ineffective	4	0	2
No answer	2	7	0
4. Perceptions of labor's influence in the Rhode Island Democratic party: [c]			
Labor more influential in the 1950's (than in the 1960's)	6	6	17
Labor equally influential in the 1950's and the 1960's	8	5	5
Labor less influential in the 1950's (than in the 1960's)	1	3	3
No answer	0	1	0
5. Perceptions of the labor–party relationship between 1952 and 1962:			
Very satisfactory	8	3	3
Satisfactory	5	6	6

TABLE 3 (cont.)

PERCEPTION/ASSESSMENT	NUMBER OF RESPONDENTS		
	Democratic Legislators 15	Labor Legislators 15	Labor Executive Board Members, 25
Unsatisfactory	0	0	1
No answer	0	1	0
Very satisfactory to 1958, unsatisfactory thereafter	2	3	10
Satisfactory to 1958, unsatisfactory thereafter	0	0	5
Very satisfactory to 1960, satisfactory thereafter	0	2	0
6. Perceptions of the labor–party relationship after 1958: [d]			
Very satisfactory, satisfactory after 1958	13	11	9
Unsatisfactory after 1958	2	3	16
No answer	0	1	0

[a] On both issues, when Democratic legislators' and labor legislators' responses were combined into a two-by-two yes-no table, there were no significant differences between them, according to the Fisher Exact Probability Test.

[b] A chi-square table was constructed in which the labor legislators' replies of "No answer" were placed in a cell opposite the answers of "Ineffective" from respondents in the other two sets. The chi-square for all three sets equalled 9.19, not significant at .05. When labor legislators were compared to labor executive board members, the chi-square equalled 8.39, significant at .05; when Democratic legislators were compared to labor executive board members, the chi-square equalled 6.22, significant at .05. When labor legislators and Democratic legislators were compared, there was no difference. Although some textbooks on statistics warn against the use of chi-square tables when more than 20 per cent of the cells have frequencies of less than 5 (see Sidney Siegel, *Nonparametric Statistics* [New York: McGraw-Hill Book Co., 1956], pp. 178–79), the test has been utilized in political science when no other means of analyzing small-sample data are available (see Alvin Boskoff and Harmon Zeigler, *Voting Patterns in a Local Election* [Philadelphia: J. B. Lippincott Co., 1964], pp. i–ii).

[c] When the three groups were compared, the chi-square equalled 7.51, not significant at .10. When labor legislators were compared to labor executive board members, the chi-square equalled 4.38, significant at .05, and when Democratic legislators were compared to labor executive board members, the chi-square again equalled 4.38, significant at .05. When the two sets of legislators were compared, there was no difference.

[d] When only evaluations of labor–party relations after 1958 were considered, and all the activists' responses of "Very satisfactory" and "Satisfactory" were combined into cells that were compared with their replies of "Unsatisfactory," the chi-square equalled 11.59, significant at .01.

majority indicated that in the event of a conflict they would support the Democratic party; 2 Democratic legislators and 1 labor legislator said that they would side with labor, while 6 and 5 of each respective group said that they would remain with the party.

The second question on Table 3 indicates a similarity in point of view between the labor legislators and the Democratic legislators on Rhode Island politics at the time of the interviews, 1964/65. Both groups offered similar assessments of organized labor's state-wide power and of its importance to the Democratic party. In each of the two sets of legislators a majority tended to feel that labor was as powerful and as important to the party as it had ever been. Along with these affirmative assessments, however, there were negative answers from a strong minority. The Democratic legislative leaders are not listed on the table, but since they were closer than the other legislators to the center of power and therefore were more sensitive to shifts in relationships, they saw the labor–party alliance differently than did the other legislators. The leaders' view was distinctly less sanguine: 4 of the leaders said that labor was as powerful as it had ever been, but 3 said that it was not; 4 said that labor was not as important to the party as it had been before, a single leader had reservations about labor's present-day role, and only 2 said that labor's position in respect to the party had remained unchanged from the 1950's to the 1960's.

The third question on Table 3 introduces the labor executive board members into the analysis. There were significant dissimilarities between them and the two sets of legislators. The labor executive board members were inclined to assess labor's over-all political activities between 1952 and 1962 in a favorable light. Of the 25 who were interviewed, 15 said that labor had been "effective" and 8 even felt that labor had been "very effective." The Democratic legislators were markedly less enthusiastic, and surprisingly, 7 labor legislators chose not to answer the question at all.[15]

When each of the three sets was compared with the others, a pattern emerged. When the labor legislators and the Democratic legislators were compared, there were no differences; apparently a legislative role channeled their perceptions in the same direction. When the labor legislators and the Democratic legislators were compared separately with the labor executive board members, however, neither set of legislators viewed labor's political activities in the same light as the labor executive board members did.[16] Once again the Democratic legislative leaders took a harder view of labor's activities than did the other two groups of legislators. Only 2 of the 7 leaders who were interviewed considered labor at the minimum "effective," while 2 said that their impressions of labor's record were at best mixed and 3 said flatly that labor had been "ineffective."

In any attempt to find out whether a political alliance has changed, it is necessary to know whether the participants in the relationship think that it has. Their assessments could be in error, but since they must act according to their own evaluations in the political world, their judgments are likely to be reliable indicators of the present or future lines of teamwork. Therefore, a study of the ways in which the activists in organized labor and in the Democratic party of Rhode Island perceived the course of labor–party relations in that state seemed to be one way of ascertaining the point that those relations had reached and their future as well. When the activists were asked if labor's influence within the Democratic party in Rhode Island was the same, greater, or less in the 1950's than it had been during the 1930's and the 1940's, they gave a completely inconclusive set of responses; the activists could perceive no distinctions. But when they were asked if they could perceive a difference in labor's influence within the Democratic party from the 1950's to the 1960's, their responses indicated an awareness of a change.

As the fourth question on Table 3 shows, the responses of labor legislators and Democratic legislators were similar.

In each set 6 of 15 said that labor had been more influential within the Democratic party in the 1950's than in the 1960's. The perceptions of the labor executive board members were much different proportionately: 17 of 25 said that labor had been more influential in the 1950's. There was no difference among the three sets, but when the three groups were compared two at a time (labor legislators and Democratic legislators, labor leaders and labor executive board members, Democratic legislators and labor executive board members), significant differences emerged. There was no difference in how the two sets of legislators perceived the labor–party relationship; a sizable number in each set found that labor's influence had declined, but a sizable number also found that it had remained roughly unchanged. When each set of ordinary legislators was compared to the labor executive board members, there was in each instance a difference.[17] Not only did the labor executive board members perceive political events differently than did the ordinary legislators, but they perceived, to a significant degree, a decline in labor's influence. The labor executive board members' view of labor's declining influence was shared by the Democratic legislative leaders; 5 of 7 Democratic legislative leaders said that labor had been more influential during the 1950's than in the 1960's.

It is conceivable that the activists in labor and in the Democratic party of Rhode Island could continue to co-operate; the difference in points of view that are indicated on Table 3 does not preclude this. It merely suggests that there was change in the labor–party alliance, that the change was perceived most strongly by the labor executive board members and by the Democratic legislative leaders, and that the change took place in the direction of lessened labor influence. If this change was perceived as only minimally harmful, that is, if the labor activists were not disturbed by it, then the labor–party coalition could be seen as likely to continue. If, however, change was not only perceived, but was perceived

as unsatisfactory by some of the other activists in the relationship, predictions about future co-operation could hardly be
optimistic.

The responses to the fifth question on Table 3 suggest
that there should be no cause for optimism about the future
of labor–party relations in Rhode Island. The range of responses is a graphic illustration of the fact that sophisticated
politicians will not allow themselves to be pigeonholed. The
last three categories of responses were suggested spontaneous-
ly, repeatedly, and emphatically by the people who were interviewed. Special attention was paid to their insistence because
their additions to the fifth question brought out a significant
difference among all of the activists in what may be the most
important political perception of all, that of how well the
labor–party relationship in Rhode Island has actually fared.
The labor executive board members felt that labor had been
poorly served. The ordinary legislators, unlike the labor executive board members, thought that labor had been treated quite
adequately. The assessment of the Democratic legislative
leaders fell in between: 3 said that labor–party relations in
Rhode Island had been unsatisfactory after 1958; 3 thought
that the alliance had been at least satisfactory throughout;
and 1 had no opinion.

The responses of the labor executive board members to the
questions on Table 3 indicate that an important element
within labor, the grass-roots leaders, perceived labor's relationship with the Rhode Island Democratic party as unsatisfactory,
especially after 1958. These perceptions tend to confirm the
impressions conveyed by the public record described in Chapter II. In further corroboration is the attitude of the Democratic legislative leaders; half of those responding did not
find the labor–party relationship satisfactory after 1958. The
attitudes of the labor executive board members and the Democratic legislative leaders taken together can be interpreted
as strong support for the hypothesis of this book, that the

once strong coalition of labor and the Democratic party in Rhode Island was changing and that the two groups were drifting apart.

The ordinary legislators appeared to have distinctive perceptions of their own, as the responses to the sixth question on Table 3 make clear: the majority of both the labor legislators and the Democratic legislators considered the labor–party relationship to have been at least satisfactory after 1958. In contrast, the labor executive board members, using the distinctions that they themselves had interjected into the fifth question, considered it unsatisfactory. Yet all of the participants were looking at the same situation, the same labor–party interactions. Whether the interactions were satisfactory or not obviously depended upon a participant's position, his role in the labor–party relationship. The labor legislators had the perceptions that were associated with the party role, not those expected of the labor role. Thus, the data shown in Table 3 substantiate Wahlke's hypothesis that a distinctive legislative role is predominant over an interest-group role. The Democratic legislative leaders seem to occupy still another position. Before their role in Rhode Island Democratic politics is examined, however, the labor legislators will be discussed further.

The Labor Legislators: Caught in the Middle

Several characteristics of the Rhode Island labor legislators emerge in this study. The labor legislators transmitted information about labor's programs to the other legislators in the Rhode Island General Assembly; they saw themselves as supporters of labor but also as Democratic party regulars; in situations of labor–party conflict they voted with the party; and they shared the perceptions of the Democratic legislators that make up a distinctive legislative role. Taking all of these characteristics into account, what political scientists call cross-pressures were likely to be the consequences of the dual claims

70

of labor and the party on the loyalties of the labor legislators (legislators who, in listing an association with labor in their biographies in the *Manual* of the Rhode Island General Assembly,[18] deliberately identified themselves with an interest group).[19]

Yet such tensions were not necessarily inevitable; the labor legislators conceivably could assume the legislative role without strain. If they did have difficulties as a consequence of dual membership in organized labor and in the Democratic party, however, they would be expected to react with feelings of bitterness or frustration toward either affiliation or both.

During interviews the legislators were asked about instances of labor–party conflict in Rhode Island because cross-pressures were most likely to be felt when there were conflicting demands from labor and the party. In assessing labor–party disputes, the labor legislators said that they had acted in much the same ways as the Democratic legislators. The labor legislators, however, offered a remarkable series of unsolicited additional responses. Seven expressed discontent with organized labor, and 3 revealed feelings of dissatisfaction with the Democratic party. Thus, two-thirds of the labor legislators expressed sentiments strongly suggesting that they had been subject to cross-pressures. Their responses were not likely to occur by chance; of 15 Democratic legislators only 2 expressed discontent with labor and only 1 with the party, a difference highly significant statistically.[20]

The feelings of the labor legislators were revealed by some of their comments. Remarking that conferences with union officials were rare, a labor legislator said, "There's no direct pipeline. They know how I feel. I don't always agree with union leadership." Another labor legislator, after describing his close co-operation with AFL leaders, recalled that "over the years I had my quarrels with some labor leaders, particularly some from the CIO." A third labor legislator remembered that early in his Assembly career he had had a run-in with a labor leader. "He threatened to defeat me unless I went along. Roberts arranged for him to apologize." A fourth labor legislator volunteered: "Labor expected too much of me; they thought I was going to get everything through the Labor Committee for them because I was a labor man. I was abused many times by labor leaders because of my independence."

In a similar vein, but with a different focus, a few labor legislators expressed uneasy feelings about the Democratic party. One labor legislator said: "The House has elected more and more conservative Democrats. There are no real liberals in the House any more. Liberalization of the labor laws has diminished because of fear of losing industry. It's afraid to make improvements. We're not a labor state now even if we were ten or fifteen years ago."

The Power of the Legislative Leaders

Aside from studies by Wahlke and his associates, little has been written about state legislative party leaders. In *The Congressional Party* David Truman examined party leaders at the federal level. He pointed out that Congressional party leaders do not possess great formal powers because the most important sanction, influence over the congressmen's re-elections, is not within their control. Still, the federal party leaders are influential by virtue of their "interstitial" position in a complicated institution.[21] They are at the center of a complex network of political communications; if individual politicians need support for personal legislation, choice committee assignments, or publicity, aid from the party leaders can be very helpful. Further, members of a party are usually in fundamental sympathy with the party leaders on issues and look to the leaders for guidance in forming their programs. Truman found that party leaders in Washington were ideologically in the center of their respective parties and therefore were well situated to exploit the resources that they had.[22]

In many state legislatures the party leaders as a group might, for several reasons, be regarded as stronger than their Washington counterparts. State legislative parties often are much stronger than the national parties because the members of state parties come from more homogeneous constituencies and tend to have, at least in some states, higher levels of party voting.[23] In Washington party leaders compete with seniority leaders who are the chairmen of the most important committees; but in many states, including Rhode Island, the party leaders are able to assume chairmanships of the most important committees.

In Rhode Island the Democratic party leaders were especially important. First, during the period from 1952 to 1962 the Speaker of the Rhode Island House of Representatives was Harry F. Curvin, an exceptionally powerful figure. His strong leadership could be attributed to various factors: magnetic personality; great parliamentary skill; a firm base outside of the General Assembly, which he had acquired as the Democratic chairman of Pawtucket; and an important voice in party endorsements for state office, which he had gained through his seat on the state Democratic executive committee. Curvin, a full-time, professional politician, has been described as being "as formidable a figure as was the awesome Speaker Cannon in the early years of this century." [24]

Curvin and the other Democratic legislative leaders controlled all initial committee assignments, all legislative patronage, and the daily legislative calendar. Further, the legislative leaders wielded the General Assembly's power over local governments as a device for bargaining with representatives; any representative who could not get legislation passed for his town endangered his nomination, and the introduction of such legislation was controlled by the legislative leaders.

In interviews the majority of the ordinary legislators—over 80 per cent of both the Democratic legislators and the labor

73

legislators—said that their primary source of information about the Democratic party's program was the legislative leadership in the party caucus. Only 2 Democratic legislators and 5 labor legislators had received information about the party's program from the governor directly, while 13 Democratic legislators and 10 labor legislators said that they had depended on the legislative leaders. Further, 13 Democratic legislators and 12 labor legislators said that they had supported the leaders' recommendations at least "frequently." Thus, in Rhode Island the ordinary legislators considered the governor to be relatively remote, even when he was a member of their own party; the party's policy was conveyed to most of the ordinary legislators by the legislative leaders in the formal setting of the party caucus. The leaders were then followed almost unanimously by the party members. Some comments from the ordinary legislators indicate the position of the legislative leaders:

Generally the bills advocated by leadership are party platform bills, so I go along. If bills are ones my constituents would approve, I approve.

Curvin had the memory of an elephant. He never forgave anything. He mellowed with years—a good Speaker of the House—a great politician and parliamentarian. You could count on his word. He was straight. You learn quickly after a few years that you can't be an individual in politics and accomplish anything.

I owe loyalty to the party. I try to make my voice heard, but I'm part of the party. Ninety-nine per cent of the times, the leadership is right.

We found out about the governor's program mostly through the leadership. When the governor was in opposition to the leadership, he would contact us directly—in secret.

Before I was a leader myself, I found out about the governor's program from the leaders. The governor communicates with the leadership.

The legislative leaders viewed themselves in much the same way as the ordinary legislators saw them. All of the leaders claimed that their advice had been accepted by the ordinary legislators at least "frequently." Most of them thought that this acceptance had been the result of explanation and discussion in the party caucus. The leaders said that they had assisted their supporters with personal legislation, especially with bills in the interest of a legislator's district, and sometimes with patronage on a small scale. Legislators who did not co-operate with the leaders were not disciplined directly, but, rather, were given no aid; the leaders simply left them alone. The legislative leaders explained their hold over the party members with these remarks:

There were no deals of any kind. . . . I would always help them with their problems—I stayed around to help.

On appointments in their jurisdiction, we would intercede with the governor. On personal legislation, we would intercede with committee chairmen to bring it out. Naturally, we tried to help the faithful.

We helped them in the House and with Senate leaders on private bills and city and town bills.

There is really no method of punishment. When we had the governor he [a rebel] just got no favors at all—not even roads or sidewalks.

The programs that the legislative leaders passed on to party members in the General Assembly came in large part from the governor. The leaders thought that the party platform had been, from 1952 to 1962, a major source of legislative ideas. They indicated that, particularly under Governor Roberts, they had received strong legislative guidance from the governor's office. Roberts would draw up the party's program, sometimes in consultation with the legislative leaders, and submit it to the General Assembly. Communications with Governor Notte were less certain, the leaders intimated, but he too had been a major source of legislation. The leaders thought that both governors had followed their advice to about the same extent, but they felt that they had followed Roberts' suggestions slightly more often than Notte's. The leaders also said that they had paid little attention to the Republican governor, Del Sesto, and that he had given little attention to their views.

A study of the relations of the legislative leaders with the ordinary legislators and with the governors of Rhode Island is useful because it provides a specific example of a legislative party, a subject that has been studied inadequately, and because it provides information about Rhode Island politics. But the primary concern of this analysis of the legislative leaders is their relation with organized labor, and in addition to the questions on Table 3, the legislative leaders were asked: "How do you decide in any given year how much of labor's program you are going to help get through?" and "What would you say the reasons are that labor got more legislation favorable to it in some years and less in others?" Their answers revealed that they saw themselves as brokers insofar as legislative demands by interest groups were concerned. In this respect they closely resembled Wahlke's "facilitators." [25] Five of the 7 legislative leaders said that labor would initiate its own bills in the legislature and that after the bills were proposed, the leaders would work out their own position. As to what their position would be, their responses ranged from remarks such as "We took what was within reason" to "We acted on the merits of each individual proposal." Several leaders said that the amount of legislation gained by labor was related to the length of the program it introduced; they implied that the more new legislation labor introduced, the more it was likely to have passed. The leaders pointed out that if labor proposed the same legislation year after year, its program would become familiar and uninteresting. Explaining his attitudes, a Speaker of the Rhode Island House of Representatives said:

When it was good legislation, I went along. They would submit their program, I would study it, and what I agreed with, I would give the green light. . . . They were very successful in the House; they ran into their snags in the Senate. This labor crowd was tough at times—they would come at the last day of the session.

Other leaders added:

They initiated it and occasionally some of it would be incorporated into the governor's program. We exerted every effort if it was part of the governor's program.

Labor has received at least as much favorable legislation here as in any other state. You can't adopt everything overnight—and they couldn't get everything in every session. But eventually, if it was basically sound legislation, it would be adopted.

Conclusions

Labor legislators, Democratic legislators, Democratic legislative leaders, and labor executive board members were found to have different perceptions of labor's effectiveness, the satisfactoriness of the labor–party relationship, and the course of the relationship over the years. These differing perceptions suggest that labor was dissatisfied with the Democratic party, that Democratic leaders were pessimistic about labor's usefulness to the party (though not unhappy with labor in any emotional sense), and that the activists closest to the decision-making level perceived a distinct decline in labor's influence in the party.

Other findings are of more concern to political scientists than to followers of Rhode Island politics. There was a distinctive legislative role, and it shaped even the perceptions of labor legislators, whose group associations were likely to cause them to feel cross-pressured. The legislative leaders, perceiving themselves as brokers in their dealings with labor, did not share all of the perceptions of the ordinary legislative role. Set apart, the leaders were a key source of information about the party program for ordinary legislators, who had only minimal contact with the governor. To obtain the high level of support that they received from the ordinary legislators, the leaders relied on general party loyalty and small favors. Not the least of their power derived from an "interstitial" position in a political communications network.

In any interest-group–party relationship, most of the important decisions will be made by the executives, the leaders at the top. In the Rhode Island AFL-CIO, a federation of other organizations, the executive officers—the president and full-time secretary-treasurer—were decision-makers, while the labor executive board members were middle-level activists. Within a state political party, the governor is likely to be the major power, as long as his party holds that office. When it loses that office, power devolves upon the legislative leadership, if the party controls the legislature. The legislators are middle-level political figures.

This chapter has examined the labor executive board members—the activists below the full-time executive level—and also the middle-management party activists, the Democratic legislative leaders. The next chapter will consider the labor executives and the political executives—the highest level of the labor–party relationship in Rhode Island.

V / THE EXECUTIVES

The labor executives and the political executives were the top leaders in labor and in the Democratic party in Rhode Island. While an executive in each group had to rely on the members of his group for support, nonetheless he had a great deal of power to act for his own organization. For this study three labor executives and a fourth person, who did not actually hold an executive position but was extremely influential within labor, were interviewed. Two political executives were interviewed also.

Labor executives filled the top leadership roles in the state labor organizations either by virtue of their positions, as in the cases of the three executives who were interviewed, or by virtue of personal influence, as in the fourth instance. They implemented the policies of their organizations in dealing with workers, other labor unions, politicians, and the general public. Because they were in the public eye, they came to symbolize state-wide labor for all of the groups with which they dealt.

Before they merged in 1958 the points of view of the AFL and the CIO were similar in some respects but differed significantly in others. The AFL, which consisted of a loose federation of craft unions, was well suited to the Rhode Island political structure of the 1940's and the 1950's. Oriented toward business unionism, it sought specific political benefits and found the personal style of the Democratic party congenial.[1] In contrast, the CIO was a tight organization of industrial unions whose members were not wholly satisfied with the existing political situation. Firmly committed to political action, CIO leaders worked for broad social and economic reforms; like the AFL leaders, however, they also wanted recognition and rewards in the form of patronage appointments to posts in the state government. The differences in outlook between the AFL and the CIO were reflected in the perceptions of the labor executive board members that were conveyed in Chapter III.

After the merger of the AFL and the CIO in 1958, the labor executives had to reconcile diverse points of view within the new organization. Merged labor in Rhode Island was like merged labor on a national scale; as the base of the AFL-CIO broadened, internal bargaining became more and more necessary for any agreement on policy to be reached. Attempts to impose uniformity always carried the risk of defection. In the election campaigns in 1960 and 1962, for example, the Electricians Union in Rhode Island independently endorsed candidates whom the state organization had not supported.

The operations of the state labor organizations in Rhode Island were distinctly small scale. Prior to their merger the AFL and the CIO each had a full-time secretary and a president; these offices were on the state organization payroll. After the merger there was only one full-time paid office, that of secretary-treasurer; the president of the AFL-CIO drew his salary from his own international union. Few material benefits devolved upon the state organizations, and there were few tangible incentives to become a labor executive in Rhode Island. For individual labor executives the rewards had to be recognition and achievement within labor and the community at large.

In the typical interest group, as Seymour M. Lipset and his co-authors described it, the leaders dominate the group because they embody formal authority and because the group members are apathetic.[2] These requirements, however, do not explain why labor executives in Rhode Island exercise the influence that they do. They have some formal authority, but beyond this they are expected to participate in lobbying and in the formulation of policy by labor executive board members, who function in the union as representatives from other organizations rather than as individuals. Labor executive board members expect labor executives to work with the political executives, who, in turn, themselves expect to negotiate with the labor executives. Little academic effort has been made to classify the leadership patterns of labor officials. Still, it seems possible to explain how these Rhode Island labor executives entered the labor movement, why they became leaders, and what their leadership styles were. Two AFL executives who were interviewed said that they had become involved in union politics as a result of both accident and ambition. They had been brought into the labor movement by the circumstances of the Depression; they wanted to advance themselves, and union office was the best available means to that end. Although these two AFL executives were personally engaging and politically adept, neither could be called a charismatic leader; for one executive, especially, the exercise of administrative skills was an important part of leadership. The career of a CIO executive, however, was motivated by a combination of ambition and ideological purposes. The CIO executive had sought advancement through union work and also had a definite program that he wanted to achieve. His leadership was characterized by a charismatic appeal to rank-and-file industrial union members. Another CIO executive seemed to have been motivated primarily by ideological concerns; he visualized the union movement and his role in it in clearly philosophical terms; and his leadership rested on forceful intellectual brilliance.

While the labor executives held the top positions in the labor organizations in Rhode Island, the political executives held the highest positions in the Democratic party. Both of the political executives interviewed had been Democratic governors of Rhode Island; one had served from 1950 to 1958, the other from 1960 to 1962. Particularly since the 1930's, the governor in American politics has emerged as a modern executive, utilizing all of the devices that are generally associated with the Presidency.[3] The governor's formal powers usually include the veto, budgetary control, and substantial authority to make political appointments. Equally, if not more, important are his informal assets: party leadership and public prominence.

Rhode Island governors were handicapped by limited control over the executive branch of the state government until former Governor Theodore Francis Green effected the "silent revolution" in 1935.[4] Green's coup gave the governorship a consolidated set of departments whose heads served at the chief executive's pleasure. Gubernatorial authority was further strengthened in 1951 with the establishment of the Department of Administration. Thus, for the period from 1952 to 1962, the governor of Rhode Island was a strong executive in terms of his formal powers.

The informal authority of Rhode Island governors was even greater than their formal authority, however, largely because of the characteristics of the Democratic party in Rhode Island after 1932. Green was succeeded by Democrats Robert E. Quinn (1936–38), J. Howard McGrath (1940–45), John O. Pastore (1945–50), Dennis J. Roberts (1950–58), and John A. Notte, Jr. (1960–62). Each of these governors was a thoroughly professional, full-time politician who had no career or outside interest beyond politics. Each had reached the governorship through a long chain of minor offices within the Democratic party and had considerable ability. Green, Mc-Grath, and Pastore went on to prominence in Washington politics; Green and Pastore served with distinction as United States Senators, and McGrath held the offices of United States Solicitor General, United States Senator, Democratic national chairman, and Attorney General of the United States.

The Democratic party in Rhode Island after 1932 was a formidable state-wide machine that operated from the lowest ward levels to the governorship and controlled all offices from city and town positions to Congressional seats. The Democrats came to power during Green's administration, but the party machine was actually built by McGrath while he was governor. McGrath anchored the party in the hands of a small group of professional politicians who were supported by a vast number of patronage workers. The Rhode Island Democratic party was most powerful under Roberts, however. Roberts had a practical and liberal outlook, was a competent administrator, and was admired for his honesty. He had gained extensive executive experience as the mayor of Providence for ten years before he was elected governor, and he enjoyed the managerial aspects of his office and was proud of his strong legislative leadership. These concerns were unusual in the acknowledged and absolute leader of a political machine that was based on patronage.

Although Roberts was experienced and competent, his career faltered in midstream. He appealed strongly to professional politicians and governmental bureaucrats but considerably less to the general public, as one might expect of a leader who had risen within the party apparatus. He was popular with leaders of interest groups that were tied to the Democratic party; from their perspective, his expertise in behind-the-scenes negotiation and bargaining and his professionalism made him an ideal party leader. But his sense of the need to maintain a public image seems to have been deficient, and the longer he stayed in office, the less popular he was with the voters.

Roberts had difficulties that might not have occurred if Senator Theodore Francis Green had not decided unexpectedly to run for re-election in 1954 at the age of eighty-seven. Roberts had hoped to succeed Green in the Senate, but instead he ran for another term as governor in 1956. He won by so small a margin that in order to maintain his position he contested the vote count. Although the Rhode Island Supreme Court declared him the winner, his judicial challenge further undermined his popularity. Roberts lost the governorship to a Republican in 1958 and in 1960, in a revealing upset, he became the first Democratic-party-endorsed candidate to lose a state-wide primary; a political unknown defeated his bid for the United States Senate.

Roberts' loss in the 1960 primary called attention to an important structural change within the Democratic party in Rhode Island. Prior to 1947 Rhode Island had no legal provisions for primaries; party nominations were tightly controlled by the party leaders, who acted through the Democratic state committee. In 1947 a law making primaries mandatory and regulating them was passed, but for the first ten years of its existence the act had little visible effect.[5] Then, in 1958, in the gubernatorial primary, Roberts' challenger obtained 44 per cent of the vote. In 1960 and again in 1962, Notte won very bitter primaries. The coalition of ethnic groups, which had been one basis of the Democratic victories in the 1930's and the 1940's, was disintegrating. Within the party there was friction between the French and the Irish in 1958, between the French and the Italians in 1960, and between the Irish and the Italians in 1962. The primaries of 1958, 1960, and 1962 signalled the end of the dominance of the Irish politicians within the party; they had controlled the party machinery ever since McGrath had organized it.

Notte can be seen as a transitional Democratic leader. Although he reached the governorship through a series of offices within the Democratic party, he lacked the broad organizational base that Roberts had possessed. Roberts had been the mayor of Providence, the largest city in Rhode Island; Notte had been the town chairman of North Providence, a small suburb. Further, Notte seems not to have been a fully developed television personality who could substitute direct appeal for organized party support. Because his 1960 victory followed a two-year Republican administration, he faced demands, immediately after his election, for patronage appointments from officeholders who had served under Roberts and also from his own supporters. In addition to internal struggles over patronage appointments and primary contests, the Democratic party was weakened by a decline in support from the voters, whose old loyalties to the party were slackening.

The Labor Executives' View of the Political Activity of Labor

When asked about the labor organizations' participation in Rhode Island politics, one labor executive from the AFL said that the AFL and then the AFL-CIO had been active in primaries, general elections, and legislative work between 1952 and 1962. The primaries included the 1958 contest between Governor Roberts and Lieutenant Governor Armand Cote for the governorship, and the 1960 contest between Roberts and Claiborne Pell for the United States Senate; in both elections labor backed Roberts. Moreover, labor helped Congressional candidates with funds that had been returned from the AFL-CIO Committee on Political Education (COPE) and also funds raised at such special events as the Labor Day picnic. These funds were allocated on the basis of a "quick decision by the officers or members of the legislative or executive committee," the AFL executive said. The amounts, while not as large as contributions from other groups—bankers, architects, utilities officials—were still, in his view, "important —substantial enough to be important."

Labor, this AFL executive said, provided workers, especially on election day; at least 75 volunteers were sent to Roberts and Notte under the direction of a labor leader: "We would go in a place of the local party organization if it was weak. We replaced the party in Pawtucket and Central Falls almost every election, particularly in 1960. We also went into East Providence, Warwick, Warren, Bristol, and Westerly. We went in because the candidate wanted us to. Roberts would ask us, or others. They were very communicative around election time about what they wanted." In this AFL executive's opinion, labor's workers were important because campaigns in Rhode Island were run so inefficiently that a few trained helpers could make a difference.

The second AFL executive interviewed, who would discuss only his personal efforts, remarked: "I always campaigned up and down the state for the party, and I was a member of the Democratic state committee."

A CIO executive said that his group had been "extremely active" in politics—in primaries, general elections, and legislative work. He remembered participation by labor in the primaries in which Roberts had run; in the 1960 gubernatorial primary between Lieutenant Governor John A. Notte, Jr., and Cote; in some Rhode Island General Assembly elections; and in one Cranston mayoralty election. He said that the CIO funds were allocated on the basis of individual relationships. Most of the contributions were given to Congressional and gubernatorial candidates, and decisions about the funds were made in meetings of national and state CIO officials. Before 1958 the amounts had been "comparatively large"; afterward they were "comparatively small." The CIO had provided candidates with a large number of workers before 1958, but with fewer afterward. For Governor Roberts the CIO workers had distributed leaflets from door to door, had stuffed and mailed literature, and had done election-day chores. The CIO leaders had made decisions about assigning these volunteers by "working with the party people." The CIO executive thought that the workers had been a help to the candidates; the Democratic party officials and Roberts had asked the CIO "for this sort of cooperation."

The second CIO executive also reported that the CIO and the AFL-CIO had participated in primaries, general elections, and legislation. He said that funds were given on the bases of an individual candidate's desirability, of the issues in the campaign, and of the closeness of each campaign. He said that the funds were relatively small, yet were "meaningful because they went to those who had less normal channels to tap. The larger ones went to those who were struggling and who had a similarity of ideology and some compassion." Roberts had received sizable contributions in his closer elections; even Notte in his first efforts had received "strong support from us." Further, Roberts in 1958 and Notte in 1960 had each been assigned 300 workers who were "extremely crucial and effective because they were not glib and polished."

The labor executives were asked how labor formulated its legislative programs and how the programs were communicated to the political executives. An AFL executive said that in the fall of each year local union officials were asked what legislation they wanted to have incorporated into labor's program. Near the end of the year a legislative committee would meet and submit a report to the executive board of the labor organization. The items that the board approved constituted the program, and "we were committed to work for its passage." Requests to include specific items in the program came more often from local union leaders than from workers, but "during the course of an Assembly session, we would have a leadership or legislative conference, and invite and report to the rank and file."

The same AFL executive explained that the labor leaders had met frequently with Governor Roberts during the legislative session. He said that discussion had been candid:

"Roberts was pretty frank with us. He let us understand what our chances were." Sometimes labor submitted written recommendations to Roberts, especially on bills that it opposed. Governor Del Sesto had also conferred with labor leaders and received their written opinions, but he was "not very frank." Labor had attempted to establish a pattern of consultation with Governor Notte, but "it was a very unhappy relationship because of an inept administration. We didn't deal with him directly." The labor leaders usually had conferences with members of Notte's staff or with his Director of Labor. Occasionally Notte would meet with the labor officials, but despite personal friendliness, he would not commit himself on issues of importance to the group.

Meetings with legislative leaders, as viewed by the AFL executive, were similar to conferences with governors, except that written opinions were submitted less frequently. The AFL executive said that public hearings in the General Assembly were not very important, but that private meetings with legislative leaders could be quite constructive. The legislative leaders required the labor leaders to defend their positions; the legislative leaders were adept at arguing against bills, especially bills that were re-introduced. It was a give-and-take process.

A CIO executive also told how labor's legislative programs were formulated. He said that affiliated unions were asked in October for preferences and suggestions; then a legislative committee reviewed all of the proposed bills and reported to the AFL-CIO executive board. The executive board decided which bills would be sponsored. Consultations followed, which had a regular pattern. First, AFL-CIO leaders would meet with legislative leaders and submit to each leader a written statement of the AFL-CIO legislative goals; then the labor leaders would meet with the governor. In his conferences with the labor officials, Governor Roberts would accept some items in labor's program, but would also indicate, with a thorough explanation, the requests that he could not support. Labor leaders had also met with Governor Del Sesto, but he had not been as familiar with labor's problems nor as liberal as Roberts. Meetings with Governor Notte, and especially sessions with his staff, had left a negative impression; Notte had possessed only a "shallow" idea of labor's aims. Meetings with the legislative leaders during the administrations of Del Sesto and of Notte had been give-and-take discussions.

The second CIO executive viewed labor's program as the result of interactions within the organization. Craft unions would offer a large number of detailed proposals, and so would county and municipal employees. At one time, all of their suggestions had been included in the program without priority or discrimination; later some effort was made to establish an order among them. Industrial unions, in contrast to the craft unions, reflected the outlook of their international union and always supported bills on broad social issues. In actually formulating the program, much discretion was left to the labor executives, but the executive board also played a "very real part." After 1955 there was a legislative committee that also evaluated the proposed bills and that eventually was given a formal status of its own.

The second CIO executive said that communications with Governor Roberts had proceeded "at one time on the basis of a selected labor group meeting with him and the leadership of both houses." During this time, the reaction of the political leaders to labor's proposals had usually been favorable. With Governor Del Sesto, however, the process had been different; there had been occasional hostility because "he didn't learn the axiom that intelligence includes tact." Governor Notte had also been difficult to deal with; he had "vacillated" by saying "yes to everything." Although labor's disenchantment had begun long before Notte was elected governor, it became more acute during his administration.

89

The Labor Executives' Perceptions of Labor's Role in Labor–Party Relations

When asked about labor's relations with the Democrats, one AFL executive considered that the usefulness of labor's endorsement of a candidate depended on the community involved. He said that endorsements were helpful in communities like Woonsocket and West Warwick, where there were concentrations of union members. He also said that labor could help candidates if it "put muscle" behind them; otherwise, "silence" was the best policy for labor to pursue. Endorsements could be important because politicians "remember if they don't get it." This labor executive perceived labor as "very effective" in its over-all political activities, and "very effective really" in working for legislation. He thought that political appointments had been important "up until merger" of the AFL and the CIO. Governor Roberts had conferred with labor leaders about appointments that affected labor, and the appointments had been cleared through the respective executive boards of the AFL and the CIO. Governor Del Sesto had not consulted labor, and Governor Notte had consulted labor but had made the appointments that he wanted to make. Roberts' administration, in the opinion of the AFL executive, had been the most favorable to organized labor.

The AFL executive described relations between labor and the Democratic party as "satisfactory up until Notte"; afterward they went "pretty much downhill." Before Notte was elected governor, labor had been "influential" in the party. It had been most influential during the 1950's, but its influence had since declined, beginning with Notte's administration. Labor's difficulties with Notte involved personalities and widened an already developing breach between labor and the Democratic party, which "hasn't been healed as yet in this state." Notte's attitude toward labor had cooled even before he was elected governor; his future attitudes had been evident at the party platform hearings. As the AFL executive explained Notte's position, "He wanted to create the impression that he was completely independent of labor. He fell for the newspaper slogans that this was a 'labor state' and that was the cause of the trouble. The die was already cast, but the Sirabella speech didn't help." Labor, the executive believed, had "played a more responsible role in the last few years in not being tied blindly to the Democratic party. We have developed broad interests in the community—constitutional revision, fair housing, consumer protection."

The second AFL executive (who held his office until 1958) said that "wholehearted" endorsement of candidates by labor was "important" because there were 75,000 union members in the state. He maintained that labor–Democratic-party relations had been "very, very friendly under my administration." He also thought that labor had been more influential in the Democratic party during the 1950's than in the 1940's or the 1930's, and that it was as influential in the early 1960's as in the 1950's.

A CIO executive assessed endorsements as "not worth anything" by themselves. What counted, he asserted, was day-to-day work done by members of labor unions. Still, he thought that endorsements were helpful when labor dealt with officeholders after elections. He said that in its over-all political activities and in obtaining legislation, labor was sometimes "very effective" and sometimes "ineffective." In its minimum-wage and anti-injunction struggles, for example, labor had achieved its goals; in other cases, it had been less successful. Governor Roberts' administrations, according to this CIO executive, had been the most favorable to labor. The executive also expressed strong feelings about labor leaders' taking political appointments: "We don't seek jobs anymore. Most of us believe that this was a lousy arrangement. Because the leadership of both unions were on the state payroll, it was our belief that their loyalty was to the Democratic party first. When new leaders—particularly from the CIO—came in, they got rid of this."

The CIO executive viewed relations between labor and the

Democratic party as "satisfactory" until Roberts' defeat; then the party began to have "many chiefs and few Indians." He thought that labor had been most influential under Roberts when it first put Notte on the Democratic party ticket and that labor's influence in the time of Arthur Devine and Frank Benti had been limited because these men had been on the party's payroll. (Arthur Devine was a former AFL president and a Director of Labor under Roberts; Frank Benti was a former CIO president and a member of the review board in the Department of Employment Security under Roberts.) He felt that organized labor had been more influential in the 1950's than during the early 1960's, and pointed out that the decline of labor's influence within the Democratic party in the early 1960's paralleled labor's decision to become independent of the party. Labor, he said, "sensed the attitude of some of the party leaders and the almost complete lack of desire on their part to make party programs useful." Party leaders mistakenly accepted the argument that Rhode Island was a "labor state" with a poor industrial climate.

The second CIO executive thought that endorsements were "very important" to candidates, and were "important" to labor when labor leaders worked with politicians after elections. He thought that labor was "effective" in its over-all political activities and in obtaining legislation. This labor executive considered himself responsible for the "fortunate" change in labor's attitude toward political patronage. At one time, he said, patronage appointments had been the prime concern in labor's political activity. While some posts were so important to labor that they had to be actively sought, the situation had reached a stage at which any post even remotely connected with labor was viewed as a political plum. In deciding to be independent of the Democratic party, labor had resolved to seek fewer appointments. The CIO executive said that without such an attitude labor could never be truly independent of the party. The executive also said that among Democratic administrations, Governor Roberts' had been the most favorable to labor.

Until 1956, in the view of this CIO executive, labor's relationship with the Democratic party had been "satisfactory," but afterward "rapid deterioration" had followed, although labor had always been able to work with that seasoned politician, Harry F. Curvin. The CIO executive thought that labor had been more influential in the Democratic party during the 1950's than during the 1940's or the 1930's, but that its influence in the community at large had been greater in the two earlier decades. He also thought that labor's influence within the party was weaker in the early 1960's than during the 1950's.

According to the second CIO executive, the labor–party relationship had changed because the politicians wanted to have absolute authority within the Democratic party, while still retaining labor's support as a legacy from the period of the New Deal. The Democratic politicians had "played the shell game in shuttling vital social legislation"; the party leaders usually did not pass legislation favorable to labor, and when they did, the number of prolabor bills was small. The Democrats often opposed labor's programs; even when they said that they agreed with labor, there was "a conspiracy among the politicians" to defeat labor's bills. As matters became progressively worse, the Democratic politicians even ignored the party platform. The CIO executive said that labor's separation from the party had been a deliberate move on labor's part, prompted by "mediocrities" and by increasing hostility within the party. Labor intended to let the Democrats know that its support was not automatic. "I hope the separation is permanent," the labor executive concluded.

The Political Executives' View of Their Relations with the Democratic Legislative Leaders

When asked about his relationship with the legislative wing

of the Democratic party, the first political executive interviewed said that Democratic legislative leaders had had only a very small role in the formulation of the party's legislative program. The program was decided upon in his own office, and the Democratic state chairman was not consulted. After the program was drawn up, the legislative leaders were invited to the governor's office, and the program was discussed and explained to them. The political executive said: "Generally, you convinced them it was sound and they would go along and support it." He described communications with legislative leaders during the sessions of the Rhode Island General Assembly as "frequent and constant."

This political executive reported that the legislative leaders had followed his advice "frequently." They never came to him with a full program, but they did meet with him to discuss particular problems, and while he rarely incorporated their suggestions into the program "specifically," he was "influenced" by their requests. He "became aware of" those legislative leaders who supported him faithfully, and he "supported them if they had abilities and ambitions." There were always some legislative leaders who were not in sympathy with his goals; these he "ignored."

The same political executive said that he had had only limited contact with the rank-and-file Democratic legislators in the General Assembly. Because they needed leadership and there were few leaders beside himself in the Assembly, the Democratic legislators were usually "enthusiastic" about his programs. They "looked to the governor" for leadership. The political executive further said that during his administrations, there had been "a great need for programs—fiscal, social, economic, in education." He said that his "programs were so strong" that the few legislators who did not go along with them did not matter.

The second political executive interviewed also said that Democratic legislative leaders had had only a minor role in the formulation of the party program; the program was evolved in his own office, and the state party chairman participated in the process.(A member of the governor's staff added that the program had been put together from the party platform and from research carried out by a committee of lawyers, and that it had first been approved by staff members and then sent to the governor.) The second political executive said that he had been supported by Democratic legislative leaders "frequently"; over 80 per cent of his "administration bills" had been passed during his second year in office. He had met with the legislative leaders once a week or once every two weeks during the Assembly sessions, and he had acceded to their requests "frequently" or "sometimes."

This political executive claimed that he had examined all private bills carefully. When a private bill was introduced by a legislator who had backed his program and when the bill was advantageous to the community at large, he had willingly signed it. He said that he had tried to apply these criteria to bills proposed by legislators who did not support him, but if the legislators seemed to be proposing "pet bills," he had vetoed them.

The Political Executives' Relations with Labor

The first political executive interviewed said that he had received information about labor's program from the top labor leaders: Edwin C. Brown, Lawrence H. Spitz, Thomas Policastro, Arthur Devine, and Thomas F. Kearney. He also said that during his administration labor had been interested in "workmen's compensation and other types of benefit legislation." He had met frequently with labor officials and, on the basis of their talks, had proposed legislative solutions to labor's problems. He claimed that he had often brought together labor leaders and representatives of industry to work out policies. He also claimed that a large number of prolabor bills had been passed in certain years during his administrations because there was "a greater need" for legislation, and "we had the leadership that was obviously lacking in subsequent administrations."

In discussing patronage posts given to labor, this political executive said that he had appointed his Director of Labor on the basis of that individual's activity in the Democratic party, not because he was the president of the state AFL. In any case, the executive pointed out, the precedent of giving appointments to labor had been set by former Governor Theodore Francis Green. Although the Director of Labor had primarily administrative responsibilities, this political executive also used him as a liaison between himself and the AFL, but not as a liaison with the CIO. The president of the state CIO also held a state office—a seat on a review board—but it was not used politically. The CIO president had been appointed to his post because labor was entitled by law to one position on the review board. The political executive did "not essentially" seek out labor men to appoint; rather, the state labor organizations "sometimes recommended people for appointment" to him.

This political executive said that he had had no personal part in persuading his Director of Labor to resign from the AFL presidency so that the AFL and the CIO could agree on terms for their merger. Further, he rejected the suggestion of one observer, that rivalry had made it easier for him to bargain with each labor group before the merger. The political executive said: "Our liaison was because of common interest on economic and social matters—hospitals, taxes. Our objectives were mutual and common." Labor had endorsed him and had provided funds and workers during his campaign. He was uncertain as to how labor's support had affected his election, however, since workers, like any other citizens, voted on the basis of economic interests.

The second political executive interviewed had had considerable difficulty with organized labor even before his term as governor. "My troubles with labor started when I was Lieutenant Governor," he said. He pointed out, however, that at one time his relations with labor had been excellent, and that labor had "fought hard" for him when he was seeking the Democratic party's endorsement, along with twelve others, as a candidate for the office of Secretary of State. He said that labor's help had been "important" to him in the state Democratic committee and in creating his public image. He maintained that labor had not been responsible for his ultimate close defeat, even though he was the first Democrat to whom it had denied endorsement in many years. The political executive thought that he had been "defeated by little groups of Democrats."

The same political executive reported that he had been informed of labor's legislative goals in meetings with the AFL-CIO executive committee. He also said that he had considered the labor plank of the party platform, which had been adopted on the advice of the AFL-CIO, as a guideline. He had conferred with labor leaders in his office and reviewed their proposals with his own budgetary officers to determine which of the proposals could be incorporated into his legislative program. A member of the governor's staff, who was not on good terms with labor, said that some disagreements had grown out of the legislative conferences between the governor and labor executives. The governor's policy was to give the labor leaders "anything they legitimately asked for," but not to accept all of their bills as administration bills. Thus, bills for minimum wages and cash sickness benefits were accepted as administration bills, but an antistrikebreaking bill was not. The governor would sign nonadministration bills, but he would not sponsor them. The labor executives were dissatisfied with this arrangement. Further, according to the staff member, the question of which labor bills would be backed by the administration was made difficult by the AFL-CIO's desire to have "everything at once." Labor had come before the Democratic state party's platform committee with eight single-spaced typewritten pages of legislative proposals at a time when the party was anxious "to simply avoid rocking the boat." Before he rewarded labor for its help, the governor had wanted time to solidify his position after the election; labor, however, had wanted its rewards immediately. The staff member described labor's bills as products of "scarred battlefields," representing only narrow interests and almost "individual causes."

In explaining his difficulties with labor, the second political executive said that he had proposed a state income tax that was to be accompanied by a one-cent reduction in the sales tax. According to the political executive, labor had advocated the tax in principle for some time, but had insisted on a sales tax reduction of one and one-half cents. The executive's fiscal advisors told him that a one-and-one-half-cent reduction was impossible. Therefore, he did not accede to labor's terms, and as a result, labor refused to support his program. The executive thought, nonetheless, that lack of support from labor had contributed less to his defeat on the tax issue than opposition from influential business groups and from the *Providence Journal*. He felt that he had been simply "clobbered." (His staff member remarked, however, that the governor had been "particularly sensitive" to, and "deeply disappointed" by, labor's refusal to go along with his tax proposal.)

The second political executive also had disagreements with labor over political appointments. He appointed as Director of Labor a man with no labor affiliation and said that he had done so because the AFL-CIO was bitterly divided internally. Since some labor leaders had wanted Arthur Devine reappointed to the post but others were opposed, the political executive had consulted the National Labor Relations Board in Washington and had decided upon a trained labor lawyer. The executive pointed out that this appointment had been widely praised in the community. The executive also said that labor had brought pressure to bear on him to make few appointments aside from that of Director of Labor. When he had been asked by labor to reappoint Elizabeth Nord to her seat on the Board of Review in the Department of Employment Security, he had done so.

The Political Executives' Perceptions of Labor–Party Relations

The first political executive assessed labor as having been "effective" in its legislative activities. When asked about labor's over-all political effectiveness, he replied: "It is hard to evaluate because so many people in labor were basically Democratic and voted Democratic." He said that until 1958, the last year of his administration, the labor–party relationship had been "very satisfactory" and that labor had been "influential" in the Democratic party. This political executive thought that the labor–party relationship had changed since 1958, however, and he attributed the change to the fact that workers now "voted like other citizens vote." According to the executive, labor's influence in the party had been unchanged from the 1930's through the 1950's, but thereafter it declined, and labor had been more influential during the 1950's than during the early 1960's.

The second political executive said that labor had been "very effective" in its legislative activities, despite some obstacles. The Speaker of the Rhode Island House of Representatives, Harry F. Curvin, had strongly supported labor in the House, but Francis P. Smith, the senator from Woonsocket, had been a formidable roadblock to labor in the state Senate. Even when Frank Sgambato, the senator from North Providence and an AFL official, was chairman of the Labor Committee, organized labor had had difficulties in the Senate. The political executive thought that the AFL-CIO Committee on Political Education (COPE) had been very effective in reaching union members when it had first been organized. Curvin, who came from a competitive district, had been helped greatly by COPE. Still, labor's influence was not impressive in state-wide elections. The political executive did not want to evaluate the labor–Democratic-party relationship as "very satisfactory," "satisfactory," or "unsatisfactory.' He observed, however, that after 1958 the labor–party relationship had changed. He said that labor leaders had been "disturbed with the party before I became governor." The AFL-CIO merger in 1958 strengthened labor by enabling it to pinpoint its objectives; therefore, in his view, the labor–party relationship had to be different after 1958. He commented that labor was "not influential" in the party in the early 1960's, but that it had some "very good friends" on the party state committee.

The second political executive thought that labor's influence in the party had reached its peak in the 1950's under Governor Roberts and had declined after the 1958 election because labor "became disenchanted" with the Democrats. He also thought that there had been a general change in the Democratic party. The Democratic party had always depended on workers for support, but it no longer represented labor only. Nor did the Republican party stand exclusively for business; instead, "both were for both." Therefore, in the 1960's, any governor had to consider the interests of all of the groups in the total population. (The staff member interviewed said that this political executive and his close associates had had "a conscious recognition" of the need to serve all groups in Rhode Island. When personality conflicts between the executive and labor leaders interfered with that policy, then "we had real hell.")

Both political executives were asked whether labor in Rhode Island was as powerful in 1964/65 as it had ever been and if it was as important to the Democratic party as it had been in the past. The first executive said that labor was not as powerful, at least in terms of votes, but that it was still important to the Democratic party because it represented thousands of people who were "basically" loyal to the party. The second executive pointed out, however, that the Democratic party had once been "comparable to Tammany Hall" in "strong party discipline and control," but had changed greatly since 1956. He felt that it had been weakened by differences among Congressional and state leaders, personal conflicts in primaries, occasional legislative rebellions, and the lack of leadership that a strong governor could provide.

VI / THE DEMOCRATS AND LABOR IN RHODE ISLAND AND IN THE NATION

The hypothesis of this book is that labor's influence in the Democratic party in Rhode Island declined during the period from 1952 to 1962. The corollaries to this hypothesis are that Democratic party leaders felt that they could achieve their goals independently of labor, that labor was dissatisfied with its future as an ally of the party, and that labor wanted to be politically independent. In Chapters II–V these propositions were confirmed by a public record of dissatisfaction and disagreement within both labor and the Democratic party and by the perceptions of labor and party activists who were interviewed.

The public record, which is conveyed in Chapter II, shows changes in the labor–party alliance and therefore supports the hypothesis. Labor–party relations were excellent during the administrations of Governor Dennis J. Roberts (1950–58);

they were strained under Governor Christopher Del Sesto (1958–60); and they were disrupted under Governor John A. Notte, Jr. (1960–62). Interviews with labor executives, political executives, and a member of a governor's staff, which were reported in Chapter V, substantiate the public record almost completely. The public record, in turn, verifies some of the points made by the people who were interviewed.

In the interviews all the categories of respondents perceived an alteration in labor–party relations, but disagreed about specific rewards and results. Labor executive board members and labor executives said that labor had helped the Democratic party in campaigns; they also said that in its over-all political activities and in its efforts to obtain special legislation, labor had been effective. When they were asked to comment on what the party gave labor in return for its support, CIO leaders asserted that after Governor Roberts' administrations the Democrats had let labor down, and AFL leaders noted a breakdown in communications with, and fewer appointments from, their old allies. Particularly strong feelings of disappointment and frustration were expressed by the AFL-CIO executives. In addition, the labor legislators, who belonged both to labor and to the Democratic party, reported that they had been subject to cross-pressures. Their remarks about their situation may be the most revealing indication of legislative cross-pressures on record.

When interviewed, the Democratic party activists agreed with the labor activists in saying that labor's support of the party had been satisfactory, but they also felt that the party had rewarded labor amply. Since the Democratic legislators were remote from the labor officials and the top leaders of the party, they could not be expected to be either enthusiastic about, or discontented with, labor. The Democratic legislative leaders, however, were frankly critical of labor although they had received more help from labor in their campaigns than had the legislators. The legislative leaders claimed that the labor leaders had been unable to produce rank-and-file union votes and had constantly demanded rewards for labor's support, but had shown no appreciation to the party for its help. The legislative leaders thought that labor had been ineffective in its over-all political activities. In their view, the ability to produce a group vote in elections was more important than the ability to lobby during sessions of the Rhode Island General Assembly.

The two political executives who were interviewed had divergent estimates of the labor–party alliance. The first executive considered it very satisfactory; labor had helped him, and the party had rewarded labor in return. The relationship seemed to him to have been based on mutual interests. The second political executive, however, said that labor had supported him originally, but had later deserted him with no good reason. This executive and the member of his staff who was also interviewed both felt that the perceptions of the labor leaders did not accurately indicate the very real consideration that labor had received from the party.

The perceptions of the party and the labor activists support the corollaries to the hypothesis. Within the party the first group to feel that the Democrats could achieve their goals with less dependence on labor were legislators; among them were many of the leaders in both houses of the General Assembly, but not the Speaker of the House of Representatives. By 1960 their attitude was shared by the governor himself. The gubernatorial staff member who was interviewed said: "The Governor realized that in order to get elected he had to serve all groups." While the party wanted to be independent of labor, labor sought to establish itself as a freer, if not entirely free, political agent. In 1958 and again in 1960 labor leaders tried to achieve independence by using two strategies simultaneously: they bargained with Republican party leaders and also attempted to intervene directly in Democratic party affairs. These tactics were not very successful, and by 1962 labor was on the verge of giving up direct intervention and of bargaining on equal terms with each party. The top labor leaders were making a strenuous effort to adopt new positions toward both parties.

The Reasons for Change in Labor–Party Relations

In attempting to find causes for the change in labor–Democratic-party relations in Rhode Island, it is necessary to go beyond the data obtained from interviews. The activists interviewed tended to explain the change in terms of personality; they observed that one individual was "just impossible to get along with" and that another was "plain tough." Personal conflicts did of course occur, but they were symptoms of other difficulties between the party and labor, just as the friendships among party and labor leaders during the 1930's, the 1940's, and the 1950's were manifestations of an alliance that was firmly based on mutual interest and agreement.

The change in labor–party relations in Rhode Island might be attributed to the broadening of the party's popular base from 1932 to 1962, particularly during the 1950's; the change in labor leadership, in the work force, and in the status of labor during the 1950's; and the moderation of the outlook and attitudes of the Republican party that resulted in a wider appeal to voters in gubernatorial elections and, eventually, in an appeal even to labor.

When any political party starts out in a minority position, it is likely to have an enthusiastic core of supporters who are united by common interests. As the party gains power, however, it is likely to attract people with diverse outlooks and interests. The process can take many years. In expansion the party loses much of its cohesion; its original groups are challenged, displaced, or simply reduced in influence. This shift seems to have taken place within the Democratic party of

Rhode Island, and it affected labor especially. The graph that follows shows the occupational distribution of the Democratic legislators in the General Assembly and illustrates the process. It shows that among the legislators the number of labor officials and workers was declining while the number of small-business-men and professional people was increasing. In the legislative party labor was eclipsed by small-business interests while, at the same time, the executive party was increasingly domi-nated by professional men. The Democratic party could not satisfy the goals of every group, and in the process of internal realignment, labor, which had been among the party's original supporters, was relegated to a lesser, although not negligible, position.

While the structure of the Democratic party was changing, so was the situation of organized labor. When the labor–party alliance was established in the 1930's under the governorships

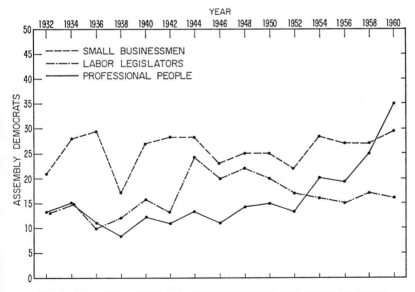

THE OCCUPATIONAL DISTRIBUTION OF THE RHODE ISLAND GENERAL ASSEMBLY DEMOCRATS, 1932–1960

of Theodore Francis Green and J. Howard McGrath, the workingman was in a precarious position. Industrial production, especially of textiles, was declining, and employers were opposed to the organization of labor unions. The employers supported the Republican party, and before the Depression a sizable number of workers did also.[1] During the Depression, however, many workers who had customarily voted Republican became Democrats.[2]

By the mid-1950's the worker's position had changed. Although Rhode Island continued to have a high unemployment level and continued to suffer from a decrease in textile jobs, the employed worker earned good wages and was guaranteed security by his union membership. Under these comparatively improved circumstances, workers tended to vote less on economic or class grounds and more in accordance with the motives of other citizens. Thus, in the Presidential elections of 1952 and 1956 Eisenhower's personality appealed as strongly to union members in Rhode Island as it did to working-class families in other states. Without the workers' votes, Eisenhower could not have carried Rhode Island in 1952 and again in 1956.

Just as the economic situation improved sufficiently for union members to be relieved of the insecurities that motivated them to follow the political advice of their leaders, the leadership of the Rhode Island labor movement became more assertive. It is conceivable that the labor–party alliance could have been sustained under the leadership of the AFL officials who were very influential during Governor Roberts' administrations, even though the party leaders were aware that the voting patterns of the union membership were changing. The AFL was oriented toward patronage and was sympathetic with the small-business interests of the Democratic legislators. After the merger of the AFL and the CIO in 1958, however, labor was dominated by CIO leaders who were concerned primarily with social reform. This interest carried labor in a direction that could lead only to collision with the party. The CIO leaders tried to groom their own party politician, John A. Notte, Jr., but failed. When Notte became governor he was unable to reconcile labor's requests with its position as only one of the many vocal, politically involved interest groups in the state and as a group that was losing control over its own constituency.

The changes in the Democratic party and in labor in Rhode Island during the 1950's were accompanied by a change in the Republican party. At one time the Republican party had been a formidable political machine that appealed to all segments of the total population and dominated state politics.[3] Its failures during the 1930's and the 1940's were the same as those of the party nationally. In Rhode Island, however, the party was severely handicapped by its association with narrow business interests and by its unwillingness to recognize the ethnic groups that were rising in the population and that were politically aware. The latter failure was surprising in a party that had endorsed a French-speaking governor as a front for Yankee bosses at the turn of the century. During the 1950's the party tried to increase the number of its supporters by appealing to more groups and by moderating some of its more stringent positions on economic issues. Its movement toward the political center was signalled by the nomination of Christopher Del Sesto as the Republican gubernatorial candidate in 1956, 1958, and 1960. Del Sesto was an experienced and articulate Italo-American politician who had formerly been a prominent and promising member of the Democratic party.

The transformation of the Republican party only began with the endorsements of Del Sesto, but its direction for the future was evident. The changes that were beginning to take place in the party had two consequences that are important to this book: as the party reconsidered its public image and selected appealing candidates, it regained some of its former attraction for working-class voters, and it became a political group that labor could at least consider co-operating with. By 1962 the Republicans were sufficiently moderate in their attitude toward labor for labor to choose not to endorse a Democratic candidate for governor.

In the 1962 gubernatorial election the Republican candidate, John H. Chafee, defeated John A. Notte, Jr., by a majority of less than 400 votes. In Chafee the Rhode Island AFL-CIO found a Republican with whom it could be comfortable. Chafee signed the antistrikebreaker bill that had been twice vetoed by Del Sesto, and he took the AFL-CIO secretary-treasurer, Edwin C. Brown, with him on a much publicized tour of nine other states to find ideas for new industries for Rhode Island. The Governor was even rumored to be developing close personal ties with a number of high-ranking labor officials. Nonetheless, in the 1964 gubernatorial election the AFL-CIO executive board endorsed a Democrat, Lieutenant Governor Edward P. Gallogly, over Chafee in a vote of 21 to 6. (In 1960 the board had refused to endorse Gallogly for the office of lieutenant governor.)[4] Chafee said that he was "confident" that he would "receive the overwhelming support of the union's membership on election day."[5]

During the gubernatorial campaign there were few visible signs of activity from labor. Gallogly's campaign was smoothly managed by a professional advertising firm, but it had little impact on the public. Meanwhile, polls showed widespread support for Chafee in all of the economic groups in the total population. The election resulted in an overwhelming defeat for both labor and the Democratic party; Chafee won by an unprecedented 90,000 votes in what was otherwise a record Democratic year. The Democrats were made painfully aware of how little effect a labor endorsement could have. In an obvious move to prevent a repetition, labor announced soon after that in the future a special committee would consider endorsements before the AFL-CIO executive board committed itself. This move was successfully led by those who had supported the endorsement of Gallogly.[6] It was obvious that despite labor's endorsement of Gallogly the majority of union members, along with every other identifiable group in the population of the state, had voted for the very popular Republican governor.

From 1964 to 1966 labor appeared to be making an effort to work with both the Republican governor and the Democratic leadership in the legislature. It is beyond the scope of this book to examine in detail the goals and achievements of labor and the political parties for this period; however, labor was a markedly less visible political group than it had been during the 1950's and the years 1960–62. Neither the Republicans nor the Democrats appeared to be courting labor or quarreling with it. The Democratic party, meanwhile, was undergoing a complicated process of disintegration that directed much of the political energy of the activists to internal affairs. Within the party a gap was widening between the legislative wing and what remained of the executive wing. Democrats serving as mayors, as members of the state committee, and as Congressmen were concerned with recapturing the governorship. These executives differed in outlook, goals, and temperament from the Democratic legislators, for there were indications that the legislative party had reached a *modus vivendi* with the affable Republican governor, Chafee, and was happy with things as they were.

In the 1966 elections labor endorsed the Democratic ticket, despite warnings from some of its own officials.[7] There were no signs, during the campaign, of activity from labor to help the Democratic candidates, and the campaign was a nadir for the party in the post-Depression era. Governor Chafee was re-elected by a slightly larger margin of votes than he had had in 1964, and he carried two Republican general officers with him. Polls and voting studies showed that, as in

1964, he had had the support of voters from all economic groups in the population of the state. Further, a signed advertisement of support from "Labor for Chafee" had appeared in the *Providence Journal;* this endorsement overshadowed any effort that labor leaders had made in behalf of the Democratic gubernatorial candidate.[8] Within the Democratic party the top officials were preoccupied with their own difficulties and expressed virtually no reaction to labor's useless verbal endorsement. Union members had obviously not followed the political advice of the union leaders, and after the election labor announced, as it had in 1964, that the AFL-CIO executive board would make no endorsements in the future without assured rank-and-file support. The Democrats turned to their own problems as the chairman of the state committee promised a complete overhaul, and the Republican party, having gained the confidence of the people, was enjoying its new popularity, at least at the executive level. In 1966 the political environment of Rhode Island was characterized by a very high employment rate, independence of union members in voting, ineffectiveness on the part of organized labor, Republican resurgence, and Democratic decline.

A recent event illustrates the far-reaching changes in Rhode Island politics. Labor's pride had long been John Fogarty, a union bricklayer who had been elected to Congress in 1940. During his terms as a Congressman, Fogarty had remained close to organized labor in the state and in Washington. When he died suddenly in January, 1967, labor leaders hoped that another unionist would take his place. Because Fogarty had won his elections by as many as 100,000 votes, labor and the Democrats alike regarded his seat as safe. Party leaders found themselves in a difficult situation, however. Twenty-two prospective candidates offered themselves for party endorsement; among them was Edwin C. Brown, the secretary-treasurer of the AFL-CIO. Mayor Joseph A. Doorley of Providence, an influential and very popular Democrat, decided not to run.[9] Brown, in turn, found little backing; private party polls showed him to be exceedingly weak in voter support. Perhaps in desperation, some party leaders supported Walter ("Salty") Brine, a local television personality.

The endorsement was won by State Senator Robert C. Tiernan, who subsequently defeated former Governor John A. Notte, Jr., in a primary.[10] Tiernan had never had good relations with labor, and the unions endorsed neither him nor his Republican opponent. Thus, despite its claim to Fogarty's seat, labor was largely ignored by the Democrats and responded in kind during the campaign. Tiernan did win the election, but only by 313 votes. His narrow victory hardly gave the Democratic party cause to be optimistic about the future of labor–party relations.[11]

The Future of Labor–Party Relations in Rhode Island

It is unlikely that either the Democratic party or labor will be able to restore the conditions that made their alliance possible during the period from 1932 to 1956; the old coalition based on mutual interest and mutual exchange of benefits will probably not be re-established. When labor endorses candidates in the future, it will probably do so only to back an already successful politician or to reward an unusually loyal supporter. Labor's legislative efforts will continue unabated, but its relations with the legislative wing of the Democratic party are likely to be uneven. Labor will probably not be able to establish close ties with any Democratic governor in the future, and the focus of its political activity will probably shift from party politics toward community-oriented civic affairs.

In the future Democratic candidates may seek help from labor, but at the gubernatorial level there will probably be few, if any, concerted efforts to obtain labor's backing. Support from labor will probably not be refused, but it will not be sought or considered important. It is likely that in the state government both the executive and legislative wings of the party will treat labor as one of many groups deserving consideration, but the party will not give labor leaders special deference in personal relations or in the dispensation of various honorary posts. Further, the party will probably continue to modify its oratory and positions to make them acceptable to parts of the business community. In general, too, Democratic candidates for state offices will probably concentrate on the new television techniques of mass appeal to voters; this accelerating trend will reduce further electoral reliance upon coalitions of groups.

Generalizations about Labor and Party Activists

One of the aims of the new behavioral science is to create a set of lower-range propositions about politics that can be tested and ultimately combined into middle-range theory. From the data in this book a number of conclusions emerge that are relevant to group behavior, party behavior, and group–party relationships. Although some of them may seem obvious, none is self-evident. The propositions represent the type of findings that can be established only by empirical investigation, the method used in obtaining the data for this study.

The data indicate that the labor executive board member was likely to be a full-time union bureaucrat whose major concern was the day-to-day administration of his own local union's business. The labor executive, on the other hand, was likely to devote his efforts to community relations, state politics, and, probably, union politics; he expected to represent organized labor in relations with political leaders, and the members of his state labor organization apparently expected him to do so. AFL and CIO unionists had noticeably different attitudes toward politics and participation in politics; the differences in their attitudes are revealed by their perceptions of political relationships. The data show that the labor legislator had a dual role in the Rhode Island General Assembly; he voted as a Democrat, but at the same time he was responsible for conveying messages from labor to the other legislators. As a result of his membership in both labor and the party, the labor legislator felt cross-pressured. If the labor legislator was typical of all group-associated legislators, then all the various elements within a legislative party could be expected to vote as party regulars, rather than as members of an interest group, and to perceive themselves as such.

Recruitment of the Democratic legislator was often by co-optation. He received most of his information about party programs from the Democratic legislative leaders in party caucuses. He voted as a party regular and perceived himself as a member of a distinctive legislative party whose contact with the governor was maintained primarily by the legislative leaders.

The legislative leader usually came from a family that was interested or involved in politics, and he belonged to the ethnic group that was dominant within the party at the time. He perceived himself as having attained to his position because of ability and ambition, not by virtue of seniority. The legislative leader mediated between the governor and the ordinary legislators, who had only minimal contact with the chief executive. He supported a party program that had been derived largely from items in the party platforms and from items proposed by the governor, and he communicated the program to the Democratic legislators in party caucuses. The legislative leader regarded most legislators as party regulars; he tried to reward co-operation tangibly and to censure defection by withholding rewards.

The political executive was likely to have a higher level of education than other members of the party. He was an exceedingly experienced career politician who considered it his role, as governor, to originate and develop a program that would be passed along to the Democratic legislative leaders.

The political executive dealt largely with the leaders and expected to reward them for their co-operation. His contact with the Democratic legislators was minimal.

The data in this book indicate that the leaders of both labor and the Democratic party expected to deal with each other. Access was unrelated to outcome; at the lowest point in labor–party relations, labor officials had no difficulty in meeting with party leaders. Some findings suggest that there was a connection between role and attitude among activists in the labor–party alliance. Thus, labor legislators and labor executive board members had distinctly different attitudes toward some aspects of politics, while different attitudes toward other aspects were expressed by labor executive board members on the one hand and by labor legislators and Democratic legislators on the other.

The labor legislators, who were subject to cross-pressures, most strongly perceived a change in the labor–party relationship and a decline in labor's influence in the party. The Democratic legislators, who had the least direct contact with the top leadership of labor and the party, were least aware of any change in the labor–party alliance. It is possible that in their case there was a time lag in awareness of political change or that, because of their position in the relationship, they would never have the same perceptions as some of the other activists. The closer to the decision-making levels in both the party and labor, the sharper and the more calculating the appraisal of the relationship. The Democratic legislative leaders were therefore harsher than the Democratic legislators in their assessments of labor's influence on the party, and the labor executives analyzed the party more critically than did the labor executive board members.

The Democrats and Labor on a National Scale

The alliance of labor and the Democratic party on a national scale was established in the 1930's, but it has tended to disintegrate as labor and the party developed their own strengths and weaknesses. Labor's resources have at best stabilized and at worst diminished since the days of the great organizing drives.[12] The stabilization of labor's position has been manifested in several ways. Since the mid-1950's the membership of labor unions has not increased as the general population or the number of employed persons has increased. Moreover, labor's efforts to attract a larger number of white-collar workers have been only partly successful, and its force as a social movement seems to have declined. Since labor is clearly no longer an underdog group but a rich and powerful interest, some of the sympathy that it once had from the public may have dissipated. In addition, the national labor leaders have not been able to aid leaders of individual unions in coping with automation; indeed, labor's national leadership has appeared to be aged and ineffectual, especially in comparison with industry, government, and university leadership. Finally, the merged AFL-CIO has at times been close to dissolution.

While labor has had problems, the Democratic party has managed to survive at least the Eisenhower years (1952–60) without losing its appeal to the nation's voters. It is still the majority party according to the sentiments of the total electorate, and the advantage that it gained during the period of the New Deal has increased somewhat.[13] In the 1964 Presidential election it even managed to broaden its base of supporters because the Republicans chose a candidate with exceptionally narrow appeal. Although by 1967 President Lyndon Johnson's popularity had declined substantially from its peak in 1964, the Democratic party's support remained stable at the very least. As it reached majority status, the party had been able to absorb portions of many groups, including representatives of business. The national Democrats were in many ways more liberal than the Rhode Island Democrats; like the Rhode Island Democrats, however, they had considerably modified the language, positions, and out-look they held in the 1930's, to appeal to anyone near the political center.

The most apparent difference between national and Rhode Island politics has been in the attitudes of the national Republican party and the Republican party in Rhode Island during most of the early 1960's. In the 1950's the national Republicans tried with some success to win labor's support; studies show that Eisenhower had considerable appeal for union members.[14] After his election in 1952 he appointed a Secretary of Labor from the AFL-CIO; when that appointment did not work out he assigned James P. Mitchell, a respected administrator with a business background, to the post. Mitchell proved to be both successful and popular. Nonetheless, from 1960 to 1966 the Republican party rejected the Eisenhower approach to both labor voters and organized labor. The Goldwater wing dominated the party.

As long as the Republicans rejected the Eisenhower approach, the Democrats, who were already stronger than labor in terms of group support, could have continued backing from labor without needing to offer the concessions that had been forthcoming in the past. Thus, at the height of their strength, in the first session of the Eighty-ninth Congress, the Democrats watched with little visible dismay as labor's most important legislative goal—the repeal of Section 14b of the Taft-Hartley Act—was filibustered to death by a tiny and usually ineffectual Republican minority. In the large coalition that the Democrats then managed, President Johnson saw no need to lend labor increased political support in order to fulfill its demands; he viewed labor as only one group among many and as a group not courted by the opposite party, at that.[15]

The case of Rhode Island gives rise to several speculations about the future of labor–party relations. For the purposes of this analysis, several assumptions about organized labor have been made. It has been assumed that organized labor was permanently stabilized in organizational development and that in the future much of its energy will probably be devoted to internal problems. For this study the scope of organized labor's political activities has been assumed to be stabilized also. Further, it has been taken for granted that union members will not revert to their former voting patterns but will vote as they have voted in recent years, without following the advice of union leaders.

Immediately after the 1964 election it was conceivable, although unlikely, that the Democrats would control the government with the support of a virtually complete national consensus.[16] Had this situation continued beyond the 1966 elections, labor would have been only one of many interest groups among Democratic allies, and labor would have received consideration as such—consideration very different from what labor received from the Democrats nationally and in Rhode Island during the 1930's, the 1940's, and the early 1950's, but very similar to what it received from the Rhode Island Democrats from 1958 to 1962. Indeed, such a situation clearly did exist from 1964 through 1966.

The results of the off-term 1966 elections indicated a possible Republican resurgence. Republican strength was too dispersed, however, for a definite prediction to be made about the party's future course of action. If the Republicans should re-adopt the attitudes of the Eisenhower years and nominate candidates with a moderate outlook and broad appeal, they might well repeat the Rhode Island experience. In that case they would have to show a mild benevolence toward labor's goals in government and an outright interest in the votes of union members. Under these circumstances, labor would have two options: it could consider bargaining with the national Republican party and make experimental moves in such a direction, or it could wait to see what the Democrats would offer. The latter possibility might entail a rather long

119

wait, during which enthusiastic Republican candidates could win a large number of union members' votes from under the very noses of the labor leaders.

These speculations lead to the conclusion that to a certain degree the course of labor–party relations in Rhode Island has been duplicated nationally. Labor's influence in, and its importance to, the Democratic party was less in 1967 than it had been in the past—less to the party of the triumphant Johnson years, 1964/65, and less as well to the more subdued and divided party after 1966. Tangible signs that labor was considering co-operation with the Republican party, a course that might be attractive to the pragmatists in labor, were not visible in 1967. For the leaders of the Democratic party signs of restlessness from labor might cause some nostalgia, but no alarm, as the Rhode Island experience has shown.

APPENDIXES

A / SAMPLING TECHNIQUES

For certain categories of respondents, interviewees were selected on a completely arbitrary basis for an obvious reason: in interviewing elites, one seeks the prominent. Labor executives and political executives fell into this category. The persons selected for other categories were from nonelite groups; that is, they were sought out because of their group characteristics rather than their personal prominence. In certain categories, therefore, weighted random-sampling methods were utilized. Labor executive board members, labor legislators, and rank-and-file Democratic legislators fell into this category. Finally, Democratic legislative leaders were treated as a blend of elite and nonelite in terms of selection.

The names selected by the random-sampling method were drawn in the following manner: year lists of all the persons who fitted into a category were compiled and combined; thus, if there were six lists and an individual qualified for inclusion each year, his name would appear six times and his chance of being selected would be six times as great as the chance of a person who was only on one list. The lists, in other words, were inclusive and weighted. As a consequence, for example, labor executive board members and Democratic rank-and-file legislators who had held their positions longest had the greatest chance of being selected in the sample. Once the weighting was completed on the lists, every entry on the compiled list was given a number, and names were drawn by using a table of random numbers: a number selected at random was matched with a number on the list, and that name and all of its other entries were removed.

B / QUESTIONNAIRE USED IN INTERVIEWS WITH LABOR EXECUTIVE BOARD MEMBERS

I am interviewing you as part of the research for my doctoral dissertation. Your answers to my questions will be kept completely confi-

123

dential, and I would appreciate your being frank with me on all items. The interview consists of three parts: personal data, some questions about the activities of your own union and about the state AFL-CIO, and some questions about your evaluations of union activities in politics in this state.

I. Personal Background

Age_____ Occupation_____ Ethnic_____
Union_____ Joined union_____ On executive council_____
Education_____

II. Unions in Politics, 1952–62

A. Own Union

1. Do the members of your union participate in state politics as individuals?
2. Does your union participate in state politics as a union?
3. Was it active during the years 1952–62?
4. What was the form of its activities?
   a) Contributions to candidates or parties?
   b) Workers for candidates or parties?
   c) Endorsements for candidates or parties?
   d) Encouragement of union members to seek party or public office?
5. Does your union publish a newsletter dealing in any way with state politics?
6. Do the members of your union live concentrated in particular election districts?

B. The State AFL-CIO

1. Did the AFL-CIO participate in politics between 1952 and 1962?
   a) In primaries?
   b) In general elections?
   c) In the legislature?
2. To your knowledge, did it contribute funds to candidates or parties during this time?
3. What was done for candidates who were endorsed? Funds? Workers?
4. Do you know of AFL-CIO publications which supported candidates or parties on the state level?

III. Evaluations of Unions in Rhode Island Politics, 1952–62

    1. Are labor endorsements very important, important, or unimportant to the candidate's election success? Very important, important, or unimportant to labor's own influence?

    2. Would you say that the state AFL-CIO had a very satisfactory, satisfactory, or unsatisfactory relationship with the Democratic party in this state between 1952 and 1962?

    3. Was the state AFL-CIO consulted by the legislators or governors from the Democratic party between 1952 and 1962 often, sometimes, or rarely? Were there changes over time? Which administration was most favorable— Roberts', Del Sesto's, or Notte's?

    4. Would you rate organized labor during this period as very effective, effective, or ineffective in its political activities? In terms of laws? In terms of appointments? In terms of getting to see Senate and House leaders? In terms of getting to see the governor?

    5. Would you rate organized labor as very influential, influential, or not influential *within* the Democratic party during this period?

    6. Within your memory, has labor's influence changed *within* the Democratic party?

        a) Was labor more influential *within* the Democratic party during the 1930's and the 1940's than during the 1950's?

        b) Was labor more influential *within* the Democratic party during the 1950's than during the early 1960's?

C / QUESTIONNAIRE USED IN INTERVIEWS WITH LABOR EXECUTIVES

I am interviewing you as part of the research for my doctoral dissertation. Your answers to my questions will be kept completely confidential. For those answers that I might want to quote directly I will ask you explicitly if we can go "on the record." The interview consists of three parts: some questions about your personal background, some questions about the state AFL-CIO, and some questions about your personal evaluations of union activities in politics in this state.

I. Personal Background

Age_____ Occupation_____ Ethnic_____
Union_____ Joined union_____ On executive council_____
Education_____

Could you describe for me how you became interested in union affairs and how you reached the position you now hold?

II. The State AFL-CIO

1. Did the AFL-CIO participate in politics between 1952 and 1962?
   a) In primaries? Which primaries?
   b) In general elections?
   c) In the legislature?
2. Did the AFL-CIO contribute funds to candidates or parties during this time? Could you tell me the process (for instance, geographic) by which funds were allocated? The approximate amounts (large or small) for Roberts, Notte, others you may have supported?
3. Did you provide workers for candidates who were endorsed? How many workers for Roberts, Notte? How were these workers allocated? What did they do? How important were they, in your opinion?
4. Did you have any types of internal communications—such as newspapers—that might be used to inform or persuade union members throughout the state on political matters?
5. How did you decide on the specifics of your legislative program (what bills to work for at what time)? What role did the executive board play in deciding on the legislative program? What role did the local unions play in the legislative program? What role did the individual union member play in the legislative program?
6. What was the process by which you made your legislative interests known to Governor Roberts? What was his attitude toward your requests?
7. What was the process by which you made your legislative interests known to Governor Del Sesto? What was his attitude toward your requests?
8. What was the process by which you made your legisla-

tive interests known to Governor Notte? What was his
attitude toward your requests?

9. What kind of a working relationship have you had with
labor leaders who are also elected representatives or
senators? Did they introduce bills for you? Did they work
for you on important committees? Did they guide your
bills through the House and Senate for you? Has this
been a consistent pattern over time? Was it this way
between 1952 and 1956, between 1956 and 1958, between 1958 and 1960, between 1960 and 1962? Is it
this way today?

III. Evaluations of Unions in Rhode Island Politics, 1952–62

1. Are labor endorsements very important, important, or
unimportant to the candidate's election success? Very
important, important, or unimportant to labor's own influence?

2. Would you say that the state AFL-CIO had a very
satisfactory, satisfactory, or unsatisfactory relationship
with the Democratic party in this state between 1952
and   1962?

3. Was the state AFL-CIO consulted by the legislators or
governors from the Democratic party between 1952 and
1962 often, sometimes, or rarely? Were there changes
over time? Which administration was most favorable—
Roberts', Del Sesto's, or Notte's?

4. Would you rate organized labor during this period as
very effective, effective, or ineffective in its political activities? In terms of laws? In terms of appointments? In
terms of getting to see Senate and House leaders? In
terms of getting to see the governor?

5. Would you rate organized labor as very influential, influential, or not influential *within* the Democratic party
during this period?

6. Within your memory, has labor's influence changed
within the Democratic party?
   a) Was labor more influential *within* the Democratic
      party during the 1930's and the 1940's than during
      the 1950's?
   b) Was labor more influential *within* the Democratic
      party during the 1950's than during the early 1960's?

D / QUESTIONNAIRE USED IN INTERVIEWS WITH LABOR LEGISLATORS

I am interviewing you as part of the research for my doctoral dissertation. Your answers to my questions will be kept completely confidential unless I ask you explicitly for a particular question if we can go "on the record." I would like to ask you questions in three areas: your personal background, your labor experience, and your political activities.

I. Personal Background

Age_____ Occupation_____ Ethnic_____
Union_____ Joined union_____ Union office_____
Education_____ When
did you first run for political office?_____ How long have
you been in the legislature?_____ What committees
have you been on?_____

Could you describe for me how you decided to run for political office and what influence, if any, your labor background had on your decision?

II. Labor and Politics

1. Would you describe the district you represent as working class, middle class, or upper class? How many union members are there in your district? Do these rank-and-file members help you in your campaigns? How?

2. Did your local union help you in your political campaigns? (Funds? Workers? Endorsement?)

3. Did the state AFL-CIO help you in your political campaigns? (Funds? Workers? Endorsement?)

4. In the legislature, how often do you communicate with AFL-CIO leaders about their legislative program? Whom do you talk with?

5. In the legislature, what do you do to get labor's legislative program (that of the AFL-CIO) passed?

6. Do the desires of the AFL-CIO ever conflict with your responsibilities as a member of the Democratic party in the legislature? Can you think of any cases where this has happened? What do you do in a case like this?

7. Would you describe organized labor as very effective, effective, or ineffective in its legislative activities for the period 1952–62?

8. Would you describe organized labor as very effective, effective, or ineffective in its over-all political activities between 1952 and 1962?

9. Would you describe organized labor as very influential, influential, or not influential *within* the Democratic party between 1952 and 1962?

10. Within your memory, has labor's influence changed *within* the Democratic party? If so, why?

    a) Was labor more, equally, or less influential *within* the Democratic party during the 1930's and the 1940's than during the 1950's?

    b) Was labor more, equally, or less influential *within* the Democratic party during the 1950's than during the early 1960's?

III. The Democratic Party

1. How did you decide what committees you wanted to be on?

2. How do you make up your mind how to vote on a particular bill in the legislature?

3. Do your constituents contact you frequently, sometimes, or rarely on pending legislation?

4. How does the party leadership make its wishes known to you on a particular bill?

5. How do you determine whether or not to follow the advice of the leadership?

6. How did you vote when leadership interests conflicted with your labor interests?

7. Would you say that you followed the recommendations of the party leadership always, frequently, sometimes, or rarely?

8. What type of relationship did you have with the governor or governors? How did the governor or governors affect your decisions on voting? Were you in direct communication or did you find out what the governor wanted through the party leadership?

9. Is the Democratic party in this state as unified as it ever was?

10. Is the Democratic party in the legislature as unified as it ever was?

11. Is the Democratic party in this state as powerful as it ever was?

12. Is organized labor in this state as powerful as it ever was?
13. Is organized labor as important to the Democratic party as it ever was?

E / QUESTIONNAIRE USED IN INTERVIEWS WITH DEMOCRATIC LEGISLATORS

I am interviewing you as part of the research for my doctoral dissertation. Your answers to my questions will be kept completely confidential unless I ask you explicitly if we can go "on the record" for a particular question. I would like to ask you questions about your political background, your party activities, and your evaluation of the relationship between the party and organized labor.

I. Personal Background

Age_____ Occupation_____ Ethnic_____
Education_____ When did you first run for political office?_____ How long have you been in the legislature?_____ What committees have you been on?_____

Could you describe for me how you decided to run for political office, and what factors influenced your decision to have a political career?

II. The Democratic Party

1. How did you decide what committees you wanted to be on?
2. How do you make up your mind how to vote on a particular bill?
3. Do your constituents contact you frequently, sometimes, or rarely on pending legislation?
4. How does the party leadership make its wishes known to you on a particular bill?
5. How do you determine whether or not to follow the advice of the leadership?
6. Would you say that you followed the recommendations of the party leadership always, frequently, sometimes, or rarely?
7. What type of relationship have you had with the governors? How did they affect your decisions on voting? Were you in direct communication or did you find out what the governor wanted through the party leadership?

III. Labor and Politics
  1. Would you describe the district that you represent as working class, middle class, or upper class? Are there many union members in your district?
  2. Do local unions or the state AFL-CIO ever help you in your campaign for office?
  3. In the legislature, do representatives of the state AFL-CIO ever contact you about their desires? Who contacts you? How do you know what labor's program is?
  4. Would you say that you support the legislative program of organized labor in Rhode Island all the time, frequently, sometimes, or rarely? If Labor's program is in conflict with the wishes of the party leadership, with whom do you side?
  5. Would you describe the relationship between organized labor and the Democratic party in Rhode Island between 1952 and 1962 as very satisfactory, satisfactory, or unsatisfactory?
  6. Would you describe organized labor as very effective, effective, or ineffective in its legislative activities between 1952 and 1962?
  7. Would you describe organized labor as very effective, effective, or ineffective in its political activities between 1952 and 1962?
  8. Would you describe organized labor as very influential, influential, or not influential *within* the Democratic party between 1952 and 1962?
  9. Within your memory, has labor's influence changed *within* the Democratic party? If so, why?
     a) Was labor more, equally, or less influential within the Democratic party during the 1930's and the 1940's than during the 1950's?
     b) Was labor more, equally, or less influential within the Democratic party during the 1950's than during the early 1960's?
  10. Is the Democratic party in this state as unified as it ever was?
  11. Is the Democratic party in the legislature as unified as it ever was?
  12. Is the Democratic party in this state as powerful as it ever was?

13. Is organized labor in this state as powerful as it ever was?
14. Is organized labor as important to the Democratic party as it ever was?

F / QUESTIONNAIRE USED IN INTERVIEWS WITH DEMOCRATIC LEGISLATIVE LEADERS

I am interviewing you as part of the research for my doctoral dissertation. Your answers to my questions will be kept completely confidential unless I ask you explicitly if we can go "on the record" for a particular question. I would like to ask you questions about your political background, your party activities, and your evaluation of the relationship between the party and organized labor.

I. Personal Background

Age_____ Occupation_____ Ethnic_____
Education_____ When did you first run for political office?_____ How long have you been in the legislature?_____ What committees have you been on?_____

Could you describe for me how you decided to run for political office and what factors influenced your decision to have a political career? Could you describe for me how and when, after that, you became a legislative leader?

II. The Democratic Party

1. When you first came to the legislature, how did you decide what committees you wanted to be on? What was the process by which you, as a leader, decided what committees to assign members of the party to? (What is the role of the deputy leader?) Chairmanships?
2. Do your own constituents contact you frequently, sometimes, or rarely on pending legislation? On service matters?
3. Do citizens at large, so to speak, contact you frequently, sometimes, or rarely on pending legislation? On service matters?
4. How does the party leadership decide what its program will be during a particular session?
5. How does the party leadership make its wishes known on particular bills to the rank-and-file party legislators?
6. How do rank-and-file members make up their minds on whether or not to go along with leadership recommendations?

7. Would you say that most rank-and-file members followed the recommendations of the leadership all of the time, frequently, sometimes, or rarely?

8. What do you do for those who accept leadership recommendations?

9. What do you do for those who don't accept leadership recommendations?

10. What is the process by which you and the governor agree on the party program? How was this done under Roberts? Under Notte?

11. Would you say that you followed Governor Roberts' recommendations always, frequently, sometimes, or rarely? Did he follow yours always, frequently, sometimes, or rarely?

12. Would you say that you followed Governor Notte's recommendations always, frequently, sometimes, or rarely? Did he follow yours always, frequently, sometimes, or rarely?

13. Would you say that you followed Governor Del Sesto's recommendations always, frequently, sometimes, or rarely? Did he follow yours always, frequently, sometimes, or rarely?

III. Labor and Politics

1. Would you describe the district that you represent as working class, middle class, or upper class? Are there many union members in your district?

2. Do local unions or the state AFL-CIO ever help you in your campaigns for office?

3. In the legislature, do representatives of the state AFL-CIO ever contact you about their desires? Who contacts you? How do you know what labor's program is?

4. Would you say that you support the legislative program of organized labor in Rhode Island all the time, frequently, sometimes, or rarely? If labor's program is in conflict with what you feel the party can give, with whom do you side?

5. How do you decide in any given year how much of labor's program you are going to help get through?

6. When you do decide how much of labor's program you can put through in a session, what are the steps that you take to get it through?

7. What would you say the reasons are that labor got (or

would claim to have received) more legislation favorable to it in some years and less in others? What factors do you think came into play to bring this situation about, if, indeed, such a situation did come about?

8. Would you describe the relationship between organized labor and the Democratic party in Rhode Island between 1952 and 1962 as very satisfactory, satisfactory, or unsatisfactory?

9. Would you describe organized labor as very effective, effective, or ineffective in its legislative activities between 1952 and 1962?

10. Would you describe organized labor as very effective, effective, or ineffective in its over-all political activities between 1952 and 1962?

11. Would you describe organized labor as very influential, influential, or not influential *within* the Democratic party between 1952 and 1962?

12. Within your memory, has labor's influence changed *within* the Democratic party? If so, why?

    a) Was labor more, equally, or less influential *within* the Democratic party during the 1930's and the 1940's than during the 1950's?

    b) Was labor more, equally, or less influential *within* the Democratic party during the 1950's than during the early 1960's?

13. Is the Democratic party in this state as unified as it ever was?

14. Is the Democratic party in the legislature as unified as it ever was?

15. Is the Democratic party in this state as powerful as it ever was?

16. Is organized labor in this state as powerful as it ever was?

17. Is organized labor as important to the Democratic party as it ever was?

G / QUESTIONNAIRE USED IN INTERVIEW WITH FIRST POLITICAL EXECUTIVE

We are on the record unless otherwise requested. Is this procedure all right with you, Governor?

 I. Could you describe for me how you first became interested in politics and what your political activities were before you ran for state office?

 II. The Democratic Party
   1. What part did the party leadership play in the formulation of your legislative program when you were governor?
   2. Would you say that your legislative leaders followed your recommendations always, frequently, sometimes, or rarely? Would you say that you followed their recommendations always, frequently, sometimes, or rarely?
   3. How frequently did you meet with these legislative leaders?
   4. What did you do for legislative leaders who supported your program vigorously? What did you do for legislative leaders who did not support your program vigorously?
   5. What did you do for rank-and-file Democratic legislators who supported your program vigorously? What did you do for rank-and-file Democratic legislators who did not support your program vigorously?

III. Labor and the Democratic Party
   1. What was the process by which you knew what labor's legislative program would be? (Whom did you talk with? How often?)
   2. How did you decide in any given year how much of labor's program you would help to get through? When you had decided this, what steps would you take?
   3. What would you say the reasons were that labor got (or claimed to get) more legislation favorable to it in some years and less in others?
   4. What was the nature of your relationship with the Director of Labor? What were the advantages to you as governor of having the president of the state AFL as the Director of Labor?
   5. What was the nature of your relationship with the president of the CIO? What were the advantages to you as governor of having the president of the CIO on the review board of the Department of Employment Security?
   6. Was it easier for you as governor to deal with organized labor in Rhode Island because of the division of labor

into two competing groups, the AFL and the CIO? Was this a division you could utilize to your advantage in any way?

7. Did you have a role in persuading the Director of Labor to resign in 1958 so that the two federations could merge?

8. In what ways did organized labor in Rhode Island help you in your campaigns for office? (Funds? Endorsement? Workers?) How helpful and how important to you was their help? Very important, important, or unimportant? Did you seek out labor people to appoint to office? Which office? AFL or CIO members? What demands for appointments did labor make?

9. Would you describe the relationship between organized labor and the Democratic party in Rhode Island between 1952 and 1962 as very satisfactory, satisfactory, or unsatisfactory?

10. Would you describe organized labor as very effective, effective, or ineffective in its legislative activities between 1952 and 1962?

11. Would you describe organized labor as very effective, effective, or ineffective in its over-all political activities between 1952 and 1962?

12. Would you describe organized labor as very influential, influential, or not influential *within* the Democratic party between 1952 and 1962?

13. Within your memory, has labor's influence changed *within* the Democratic party? If so, why?
    a) Was labor more, equally, or less influential *within* the Democratic party during the 1930's and the 1940's than during the 1950's?
    b) Was labor more, equally, or less influential *within* the Democratic party during the 1950's than during the early 1960's?

14. Is the Democratic party in this state as unified as it ever was?

15. Is the Democratic party in the legislature as unified as it ever was?

16. Is the Democratic party in this state as powerful as it ever was?

17. Is organized labor in this state as powerful as it ever was?

18. Is organized labor as important to the Democratic party as it ever was?

H / QUESTIONNAIRE USED IN INTERVIEW WITH SECOND POLITICAL EXECUTIVE

We are on the record unless otherwise requested. Is this procedure all right with you, Governor?

I. Could you describe for me how you first became interested in politics and what your political activities were before you ran for state office?

II. The Democratic Party

   1. What part did the party leadership play in the formulation of your legislative program when you were governor?
   2. Would you say that your legislative leaders followed your recommendations always, frequently, sometimes, or rarely? Would you say that you followed their recommendations always, frequently, sometimes, or rarely?
   3. How frequently did you meet with your legislative leaders?
   4. What did you do for legislative leaders who supported your program vigorously? What did you do for legislative leaders who did not support your program vigorously?
   5. What did you do for rank-and-file Democratic legislators who supported your program vigorously? What did you do for rank-and-file Democratic legislators who did not support your program vigorously?

III. Labor and the Democratic Party

   1. What was the process by which you knew what labor's legislative program would be? (Whom did you talk with? How often?)
   2. How did you decide in any given year how much of labor's program you would help to get through? When you had decided this, what steps would you take?
   3. What would you say the reasons were that labor got (or claimed to get) more legislation favorable to it in some years and less in others?
   4. At one time, you were the political leader most admired, it would seem, by organized labor in this state. Yet, after your elections, relations between you and labor seemed to deteriorate. Why did this happen?
   5. Why did you break precedent and appoint a Director of Labor who was not from labor's ranks?
   6. Did labor's failure to support your income tax program affect your efforts in behalf of such a program?

7. In what ways did organized labor in Rhode Island help you in your early campaigns for office? (Funds? Endorsement? Workers?) Was their help very important, important, or unimportant?

8. Did organized labor's not endorsing you in 1962, in your opinion, have an important effect on the outcome of that election? Do you think the separation between labor and the Democratic party was temporary or permanent? Did you seek out labor people to appoint to office? Which office? What demands for appointments did labor make?

9. Would you describe the relationship between organized labor and the Democratic party in Rhode Island between 1952 and 1962 as very satisfactory, satisfactory, or unsatisfactory?

10. Would you describe organized labor as very effective, effective, or ineffective in its legislative activities between 1952 and 1962?

11. Would you describe organized labor as very effective, effective, or ineffective in its over-all political activities between 1952 and 1962?

12. Would you describe organized labor as very influential, influential, or not influential *within* the Democratic party between 1952 and 1962?

13. Within your memory, has labor's influence changed *within* the Democratic party?
    a) Was labor more, equally, or less influential *within* the Democratic party during the 1930's and the 1940's than during the 1950's?
    b) Was labor more, equally, or less influential *within* the Democratic party during the 1950's than during the 1960's?

14. Is the Democratic party in this state as unified as it ever was?

15. Is the Democratic party in the legislature as unified as it ever was?

16. Is the Democratic party in this state as powerful as it ever was?

17. Is organized labor in this state as powerful as it ever was?

18. Is organized labor as important to the Democratic party as it ever was?

NOTES

CHAPTER I

1. See V. O. Key, Jr., *American State Politics: An Introduction* (New York: Alfred A. Knopf, 1956), p. 4., and Duane Lockard, *The Politics of State and Local Government* (New York: Macmillan Co., 1963), chaps. i–iii.

2. Edwin C. Banfield, *Political Influence* (Glencoe, Ill.: Free Press, 1961), p. 3. See also V. O. Key, Jr., *Southern Politics in State and Nation* (New York: Alfred A. Knopf, 1949), and *American State Politics;* John C. Wahlke *et al., The Legislative System: Explorations in Legislative Behavior* (New York: John Wiley & Sons, 1962); Joseph A. Schlesinger, *How They Became Governor: A Study of Comparative State Politics, 1870–1950* (East Lansing: Governmental Research Bureau, Michigan State University, 1957); and Leon Epstein, *Politics in Wisconsin* (Madison: University of Wisconsin Press, 1958).

3. The basic studies include: Oliver Garceau, *The Political Life of the American Medical Association* (Cambridge: Harvard University Press, 1941); Justin Gray, *The Inside Story of the Legion* (New York: Boni and Gaer, 1948); Peter Odegard, *Pressure Politics: The Story of the Anti-Saloon League* (New York: Columbia University Press, 1928); Wesley McCune, *The Farm Bloc* (Garden City, N.Y.: Doubleday, Doran & Co., 1943); Dayton D. McKean, *Pressures on the Legislature of New Jersey* (New York: Columbia University Press, 1938); Stanley Kelly, Jr., *Professional Public Relations and Political Power* (Baltimore: Johns Hopkins Press, 1956); and Samuel J. Eldersveld, *Political Affiliation in Metropolitan Detroit* (Ann Arbor: University of Michigan Press, 1957).

4. See Fay Calkins, *The CIO and the Democratic Party* (Chicago: University of Chicago Press, 1952); Oliver Garceau and Corinne Silverman, "A Pressure Group and the Pressured," *American Political Science Review,* XLVIII (1954), 672–91; and John

C. Wahlke *et al.*, "American State Legislators' Role Orientations Toward Pressure Groups," *Journal of Politics*, XXII (1960), 203–27.

5. U. S. Bureau of the Census, *Census of Population: 1960*, Vol. I, Part XLI (Washington: U. S. Govt. Print. Off., 1963), pp. 41–45.

6. See Wahlke *et al.*, "American State Legislators," pp. 217–19. The best general discussion of the concept of political culture is contained in Gabriel A. Almond and Sidney Verba, *The Civic Culture: Political Attitudes and Democracy in Five Nations* (Princeton: Princeton University Press, 1963), pp. 12–29.

7. U. S. Bureau of the Census, *Statistical Abstract of the United States: 1963* (Washington: U. S. Govt. Print. Off., 1963), p. 11.

8. *Census of Population: 1960*, Vol. I, Part XLI, p. 228

9. U. S. Bureau of the Census, *County and City Data Book, 1962* (Washington: U. S. Govt. Print. Off., 1962), p. 2.

10. See Elmer E. Cornwell, Jr., "Party Absorption of Ethnic Groups: The Case of Providence, R. I.," *Social Forces*, XXXVIII (1960), 205–10; Murray Stedman, Jr., and Susan W. Stedman, "The Rise of the Democratic Party of Rhode Island," *New England Quarterly*, XXIV (1951), 329–41; and Duane Lockard, *New England State Politics* (Princeton: Princeton University Press, 1959), pp. 196–202.

11. U. S. Bureau of the Census, *Historical Statistics of the United States* (Washington: U. S. Govt. Print. Off., 1960), p. 684.

12. See Erwin L. Levine, *Theodore Francis Green: The Rhode Island Years, 1906–1936* (Providence: Brown University Press, 1963), especially p. 190, and Samuel Lubell, *The Future of American Politics* (Garden City, N. Y.: Doubleday & Co., 1956).

13. See Lockard, *New England State Politics*, chap. vii, and Malcolm E. Jewell, *The State Legislature: Politics and Practice* (New York: Random House, 1962), p. 36.

14. Murray B. Levin with George Blackwood, *The Compleat Politician: Political Strategy in Massachusetts* (Indianapolis: Bobbs-Merrill Co., 1962), p. 17.

15. For general histories, see Robert F. Hoxie, *Trade Unionism in the United States* (New York: D. Appleton-Century, 1936); Florence Peterson, *American Labor Unions, What They Are and How They Work* (New York: Harper and Brothers, 1952); Foster Rhea Dulles, *Labor in America: A History* (New York: Thomas Y. Crowell Co., 1955); and Joseph G. Rayback, *A History of American Labor* (New York: Macmillan Co., 1959).

16. Jack Barbash, *The Practice of Unionism* (New York: Harper and Brothers, 1956), p. 8.

17. V. O. Key, Jr., *Politics, Parties, and Pressure Groups* (New York: Thomas Y. Crowell Co., 1958), p. 226.

18. For the ideas of the proponents of the group-theory approach, see Arthur F. Bentley, *The Process of Government: A Study of Social Pressures* (Chicago: University of Chicago Press, 1908; Bloomington, Ind.: Principia Press, 1935); David B. Truman, *The Governmental Process: Political Interests and Public Opinion* (New York: Alfred A. Knopf, 1951); Earl Latham, *The Group Basis of Politics: A Study in Basing-Point Legislation* (Ithaca: Cornell University Press, 1952); and Bertram Gross, *The Legislative Struggle: A Study in Social Combat* (New York: McGraw Hill Book Co., 1953). Questions about group theory are raised by Peter Odegard in "A Group Basis for Politics: A New Name for an Ancient Myth," *Western Political Quarterly*, XI (1958), 689–702, and by Stanley Rothman in "Systematic Political Theory: Observations on the Group Approach," *American Political Science Review*, LIV (1960), 15–33.

19. Truman, *The Governmental Process*, pp. 33, 37.

20. *Ibid.*, p. 113.

21. For comments on this point, see Richard A. Lester, *As Unions Mature: An Analysis of the Evolution of American Unionism* (Princeton: Princeton University Press, 1958), and George R. Brooks, "Reflections on the Changing Character of American Labor Unions," in *Unions and Union Leadership: Their Human Meaning*, ed. Jack Barbash (New York: Harper and Brothers, 1959), pp. 27–36.

22. See Robert Michels, *Political Parties: A Sociological Study of the Oligarchical Tendencies of Modern Democracy*, trans. Eden and Cedar Paul (New York: Dover Publications, 1959), p. 401.

23. See Seymour M. Lipset, Martin A. Trow, and James S. Coleman, *Union Democracy: The Internal Politics of the International Typographical Union* (Glencoe, Ill.: Free Press, 1956); John A. Fitch, *Social Responsibilities of Organized Labor* (New York: Harper and Brothers, 1957); Philip Taft, *The Structure and Government of Trade Unions* (Cambridge: Harvard University Press, 1954); Grant McConnell, "The Spirit of Private Government," *American Political Science Review*, LII (1958), 754–70; and James G. March and Herbert Simon, *Organizations* (New York: John Wiley & Sons, 1958). Lipset, for example, seems to agree with Michels. See Lipset, *Political Man: The Social Bases of Politics*

(Garden City, N.Y.: Doubleday & Co., 1959), chap. xii. Sigmund Neuman, in contrast, is critical of Michels in his essay "Toward A Comparative Study in Politics," in *Modern Political Parties: Approaches to Comparative Politics,* ed. Sigmund Neuman (Chicago: University of Chicago Press, 1956).

24. See Paul Jacobs, "Union Democracy and the Public Good," in U. S. Library of Congress, Legislative Reference Service, *Government Regulation of Internal Union Affairs Affecting the Rights of Members* (Washington: U. S. Govt. Print. Off., 1958), pp. 132–38.

25. Lipset, Trow, and Coleman cite three causes of leadership dominance: the monopoly of power usually given to officials, the desire of leaders to perpetuate their own pre-eminence, and the lack of rank-and-file interest in organizational affairs: see *Union Democracy,* pp. 9–11.

26. See David L. Sills, *The Volunteers: Means and Ends in a National Organization* (Glencoe, Ill.: Free Press, 1957), pp. 3–10, for a discussion of this point.

27. The CIO organized the units which came to comprise its membership, particularly in the early phases of the Mineworkers Organizing Committee and the Committee for Industrial Organization; see Benjamin Stolberg, *The Story of the CIO* (New York: Viking Press, 1938). The AFL, in contrast, was a federation formed originally of already existing craft organizations; see Rayback, *A History of American Labor,* and Dulles, *Labor in America.*

28. Samuel J. Eldersveld, *Political Parties: A Behavioral Analysis* (Chicago: Rand McNally & Co., 1964), p. 5.

29. These concepts were originally put forth by Gabriel A. Almond in the Introduction to *The Politics of the Developing Areas,* ed. Gabriel A. Almond and James S. Coleman (Princeton: Princeton University Press, 1960).

30. Eldersveld, *Political Parties,* p. 6.

31. See Harold Laswell and Abraham Kaplan, *Power and Society* (New Haven: Yale University Press, 1950), pp. 219–20.

32. Eldersveld, *Political Parties,* p. 9.

33. See David B. Truman, *The Congressional Party: A Case Study* (New York: John Wiley & Sons, 1959), pp. 8–10, 289–319, and Duane Lockard, "Legislative Parties in Connecticut," *American Political Science Review,* XLVIII (1954), 166–73.

34. Lockard, *New England State Politics,* pp. 212–27. Party may be a more important variable in the legislative voting behavior of some states than it is in Congress. See Key, *American State Politics;* Malcolm Jewell, "Party Voting in American State Legisla-

tures," *American Political Science Review,* XLIX (1955), 773–91; and Thomas A. Flinn, "Party Responsibility in the States: Some Causal Factors," *American Political Science Review,* LVIII (1964), 60–72.

35. See Austin Ranney, *The Doctrine of Responsible Party Government: Its Origins and Present State* (Urbana: University of Illinois Press, 1954).

36. Robert A. Dahl and Charles Lindblom, *Politics, Economics, and Welfare* (New York: Harper and Brothers, 1953), p. 324.

37. *Ibid.,* pp. 272–365.

38. *Ibid.,* p. 326.

39. *Ibid.,* p. 333.

40. The basic techniques for constructing the questionnaires and for the sampling are drawn from Mildred Parten, *Surveys, Polls, and Samples* (New York: Harper and Brothers, 1950); C. A. Moser, *Survey Methods in Social Investigation* (New York: Macmillan Co., 1958); William J. Goode and Paul K. Hatt, *Methods in Social Research* (New York: McGraw-Hill Book Co., 1952); and Herbert Hyman, *Survey Design and Analysis: Principles, Cases, and Procedures* (Glencoe, Ill.: Free Press, 1955). The questionnaires are printed in the Appendix.

41. Rhode Island Secretary of State, *Manual with Rules and Orders for the Use of the General Assembly of the State of Rhode Island* (Providence: 1931/32–1965/66, all eds.).

CHAPTER II

1. *Providence Journal,* January 2, 1952.

2. *Ibid.,* January 4, 1952.

3. *Ibid.,* January 6, 1952.

4. *Ibid.,* January 12, 1952.

5. *Ibid.,* April 15, 16, 1952.

6. *Ibid.,* January 12, 1952.

7. *Ibid.,* April 12, 1952; August 17, 1952; September 4, 12, 1952.

8. *Evening Bulletin,* October 6, 1952.

9. *Ibid.,* January 6, 1953.

10. *Providence Journal,* January 15, 1953.

11. *Ibid.,* February 4, 1953.

12. *Ibid.*

13. *Ibid.,* March 11, 27, 1953.

14. *Ibid.,* April 4, 19, 1953.

15. *Ibid.,* July 2, 1953; *Evening Bulletin,* July 2, 1953.

16. *Providence Journal,* October 11, 1953.

17. *Evening Bulletin,* February 3, 1954; *Providence Journal,* February 4, 1954.

18. *Ibid.,* February 6, 1954.

19. *Evening Bulletin,* May 7, 1954.

20. *Providence Journal,* May 8, 1954.

21. *Evening Bulletin,* October 13, 1954.

22. While still in his twenties, Spitz became a union organizer. He was a founder of the Industrial Trade Union of Woonsocket, a syndicalist textile union which reached a membership of 22,000 in 1942. After the war he worked for Philip Murray of the Steelworkers Union. He attended Brown University, graduating in 1951, and was elected to Phi Beta Kappa.

23. *Providence Journal,* March 11, 1955.

24. John F. Burns, "Prospects Dim for Miss Nord," *Providence Journal,* April 3, 1955.

25. *Evening Bulletin,* April 20, 1955.

26. *Ibid.*

27. *Providence Journal,* June 12, 1955.

28. Rhode Island. *Laws and Statutes, etc. Rhode Island General Laws* (State of Rhode Island and Providence Plantations, as revised 1936, as revised 1951, as revised 1956, plus yearly supplements).

29. *Providence Journal,* September 27, 1955.

30. *Ibid.,* October 24, 1955.

31. John F. Burns, "State Merger of AFL-CIO a Delicate Issue," *ibid.,* December 4, 1955.

32. Interviews with author.

33. David M. Cameron, "Labor Witnesses Flay R.I. Wage Floor Bill," *Providence Journal,* March 29, 1956.

34. Duane Lockard, *New England State Politics* (Princeton: Princeton University Press, 1959), p. 223.

35. John F. Burns, "Five N. E. States Beating Rhode Island in Plans to Complete Big Labor Merger," *Providence Journal,* April 29, 1956.

36. John F. Burns, "AFL Endorses Sgambato for Lieut. Governor," *ibid.,* June 10, 1956.

37. *Providence Journal,* September 1, 1956.

38. John F. Burns, "R.I. $1 Pay Bill Scored by CIO," *ibid.,* April 8, 1957.

39. John F. Burns, "Roberts' Speech Indicates He Will Run Again," *ibid.,* September 2, 1957.

40. John F. Burns, "State CIO May Reveal Stand on Roberts, Cote," *ibid.*, February 23, 1958.

41. Vincent L. Lombardi, "The State Federation and State Industrial Union Council Manager in Rhode Island" (Master's Thesis, University of Rhode Island, 1961), p. 152.

42. *Evening Bulletin,* March 20, 1958.

43. John F. Burns, "Merger Presages New Era for R.I. Labor," *Providence Journal,* July 27, 1958; *Evening Bulletin,* September 6, 1958.

44. *Providence Journal,* October 12, 18, 22, 1958.

45. *Evening Bulletin,* October 23, 1958.

46. *Ibid.*

47. *Providence Journal,* October 30, 1958.

48. *Ibid.,* October 30, 31, 1958.

49. *Evening Bulletin,* November 10, 1958.

50. *Providence Journal,* January 6, 1959.

51. *Ibid.,* January 12, 1959.

52. *Ibid.,* March 29, 1959.

53. John F. Burns, "AFL-CIO to Reward Only Political Friends," *ibid.,* May 4, 1959; G. Richmond Carpenter and C. Elliott Stocker, "Feud Erupts in Senate," *Evening Bulletin,* May 6, 1959.

54. G. Richmond Carpenter and C. Elliott Stocker, "Feud Erupts in Senate."

55. *Ibid.*

56. *Ibid.*

57. *Providence Journal,* May 15, 1959.

58. *Evening Bulletin,* May 28, 1959.

59. *Providence Journal,* July 3, 1959.

60. *Ibid.,* July 13, 1959.

61. *Ibid.,* July 15, 1959.

62. *Ibid.,* September 6, 1959.

63. *Ibid.,* September 7, 1959.

64. *Ibid.,* July 19, 1959; September 6, 1959.

65. *Evening Bulletin,* October 6, 1959.

66. *Ibid.,* November 4, 1959.

67. *Providence Journal,* February 27, 1960.

68. *Ibid.,* March 3, 1960.

69. *Ibid.,* June 24, 1960.

70. *Ibid.,* May 27, 1960.

71. *Ibid.,* June 25, 1960.

72. *Ibid.,* September 2, 1960.

73. *Ibid.,* September 6, 1960.

74. *Evening Bulletin,* September 16, 1960; *Providence Journal,* September 18, 1960.

75. *Ibid.,* October 31, 1960; November 5, 1960.

76. *Ibid.,* November 21, 1960.

77. *Evening Bulletin,* November 21, 1960.

78. *Providence Journal,* December 22, 1960.

79. Interview with author.

80. *Providence Journal,* February 3, 1961.

81. *Ibid.,* February 18, 1961.

82. *Ibid.,* February 19, 1961.

83. *Ibid.,* February 27, 1961.

84. *Ibid.,* March 2, 1961.

85. *Evening Bulletin,* March 16, 1961; *Providence Journal,* March 23, 1961; April 8, 17, 20, 1961.

86. *Ibid.,* April 30, 1961.

87. *Ibid.,* May 5, 1961.

88. D. W. Griffith, "Industry, Labor Disappointed," *Evening Bulletin,* June 9, 1961.

89. *Ibid.*

90. *Evening Bulletin,* June 26, 1961.

91. *Providence Journal,* September 4, 1961.

92. *Evening Bulletin,* December 21, 1961.

93. James V. Wyman, "Fewer Work Stoppages in 1961," *Providence Journal,* January 2, 1962.

94. *Providence Journal,* January 25, 1962; February 1, 1962.

95. *Ibid.,* February 15, 22, 1962.

96. *Evening Bulletin,* April 14, 1962.

97. *Providence Journal,* April 15, 1962.

98. *Ibid.,* April 21, 1962.

99. *Ibid.,* May 7, 1962.

100. *Ibid.,* May 8, 1962.

101. *Ibid.*

102. *Ibid.,* May 18, 1962.

103. John P. Hackett, "Labor Backs None Before Primary," *Evening Bulletin,* August 17, 1962.

104. *Providence Journal,* October 10, 1962.

105. *Ibid.*

106. John P. Hackett, "Labor Noncommittal on Governor's Plight," *ibid.,* November 12, 1962.

107. *Evening Bulletin,* October 31, 1962.

108. John P. Hackett, "Labor Noncommittal on Governor's Plight."

CHAPTER III

1. The literature on labor executive board members is less extensive than one might expect. See Glen W. Miller and Edward J. Stackton, "Local Union Officer—His Background, Activities and Attitudes," *Labor Law Journal*, VIII (1957), 28–39; and Ely Chinoy, "Local Union Leadership," in *Studies in Leadership*, ed. Alvin W. Gouldner (New York: Harper and Brothers, 1950), pp. 157–73. For more general studies of local unions, see Jack Barbash, *Labor's Grass Roots: A Study of the Local Union* (New York: Harper and Brothers, 1961); Leonard B. Sayles and George R. Strauss, *The Local Union, Its Place in the Industrial Plant* (New York: Harper and Brothers, 1953); Arnold S. Tannenbaum and Robert L. Kahn, *Participation in Union Locals* (Evanston, Ill.: Row, Peterson and Co., 1958); and Joel Seidman *et al.*, *The Worker Views His Union* (Chicago: University of Chicago Press, 1958). For studies of leadership in the union, see Seymour M. Lipset, *Political Man: The Social Bases of Politics* (Garden City, N.Y.: Doubleday & Co., 1959); Lois MacDonald, *Leadership and the Trade Union Leader* (New York: New York University Press, 1959); and *Unions and Union Leadership: Their Human Meaning*, ed. Jack Barbash (New York: Harper and Brothers, 1959).

2. For a study of union leadership at the national level, see C. Wright Mills and Helen Dinerman, "Leaders of the Unions," in *The House of Labor: Internal Operations of American Unions*, ed. J. B. S. Hardman and Maurice F. Neufeld (Englewood Cliffs, N.J.: Prentice-Hall, 1951), pp. 24–47.

3. Statistically, the difference between the number of respondents who answered "Yes" to the third question on Table 2 and the number who answered "Yes" to the fourth question is significant at the .005 level of confidence on a chi-square test. This level means that this distribution of replies would be very unlikely indeed to occur by chance. To the degree that perceptions are an accurate measurement of change in a relationship, those examined here undoubtedly indicate that there was a shift.

CHAPTER IV

1. For general works on legislative bodies, see Malcolm E. Jewell and Samuel C. Patterson, *The Legislative Process in the United States* (New York: Random House, 1966), and William J. Keefe

and Morris S. Ogul, *The American Legislative Process* (Englewood Cliffs, N.J.: Prentice-Hall, 1964).

2. The definitive work on state legislators is John C. Wahlke *et al.*, *The Legislative System: Explorations in Legislative Behavior* (New York: John Wiley & Sons, 1962), in which see chap. vii. See also Duncan MacRae, Jr., "The Role of the State Legislator in Massachusetts," *American Sociological Review*, XIX (1954), 185–94, and Heinz Eulau *et al.*, "Career Perspectives of American State Legislatures," in *Political Decision Makers*, ed. Dwaine Marvick (Glencoe, Ill.: Free Press, 1961), pp. 218–63.

3. MacRae, "The Role of the State Legislator in Massachusetts," p. 185.

4. See John C. Wahlke *et al.*, *The Legislative System*, and "American State Legislators' Role Orientations Toward Pressure Groups," *Journal of Politics*, XXII (1960), 203–27.

5. Wahlke *et al.*, "American State Legislators' Role Orientations," p. 205.

6. Harry M. Scoble, "Organized Labor in Electoral Politics: Some Questions for the Discipline," *Western Political Quarterly*, XVI (1963), 666.

7. Belle Zeller, ed., *American State Legislatures* (New York: Thomas Y. Crowell Co., 1954), p. 72.

8. L. G. Seligman, "Political Change: Legislative Elites and Parties in Oregon," *Western Political Quarterly*, XVII (1964), 177–87.

9. Scoble, "Organized Labor in Electoral Politics," *loc. cit.*

10. Heinz Eulau *et al.*, "The Political Socialization of American State Legislators," in *Legislative Behavior*, ed. John C. Wahlke and Heinz Eulau (Glencoe, Ill.: Free Press, 1959), p. 306.

11. James D. Barber, *The Lawmakers: Recruitment and Adaptation to Legislative Life* (New Haven: Yale University Press, 1965), p. 173.

12. Rhode Island. *Laws and Statutes, etc. Rhode Island General Laws* (State of Rhode Island and Providence Plantations, as revised 1936, as revised 1951, as revised 1956, plus yearly supplements).

13. A Spearman rank-order correlation analysis (ranking each Assembly session according to the number of its labor legislators and the proportion of labor bills to its total legislative output) revealed no significant relationship between the number of labor legislators and the amount of labor legislation passed. The correlation was .225, very low and not significant statistically. When the

1934–62 data span was split into the 1934–48 New Deal–Fair Deal period and the 1948–62 postwar period, the results were slightly different. The first segment showed a correlation of .536 that could be interpreted as a very weak positive result, although it is not significant at .05. But then the second period yielded a correlation of .042—no correlation at all. The strength of individual bills cannot be evaluated by these quantitative devices, but they do suggest that in Rhode Island it was not the number of labor legislators that brought about labor legislation.

14. Wahlke *et al.*, *The Legislative System*, p. 333.

15. If the labor legislators' replies of "No answer" are interpreted as "Ineffective," and they are placed in a cell opposite the replies of "Ineffective" of the other two sets, there appears among all three sets a difference that is significant at the .10 level of confidence, something more than a chance distribution, but still not of great statistical importance.

16. When the labor legislators and the Democratic legislators were compared separately with the labor executive board members in a chi-square test based on Table 3, in each instance there was a difference at the .05 level of confidence.

17. The difference was significant at the .05 level of confidence.

18. Rhode Island Secretary of State, *Manual with Rules and Orders for the Use of the General Assembly of the State of Rhode Island* (Providence: 1931/32–1965/66, all eds.).

19. The concept of cross-pressures has been studied extensively, primarily in reference to voting. See Paul Lazarsfeld *et al.*, *The People's Choice: How the Voter Makes Up His Mind in a Presidential Campaign* (New York: Duell, Sloan & Pearce, 1944), chap. vi, and Angus Campbell *et al.*, *The American Voter* (New York: John Wiley & Sons, 1960), pp. 86–88. Although the main response of voters to cross-pressures was withdrawal, Robert Lane noted in *Political Life: Why People Get Involved in Politics* (Glencoe, Ill.: Free Press, 1959), p. 203, that this reaction was "only one of several means of solving the conflict problem"; another solution was "identification with one of the conflicting reference groups (sometimes because of frustration in the other)." David B. Truman, in *The Governmental Process: Political Interests and Public Opinion* (New York: Alfred A. Knopf, 1951), p. 162, applied the concept of cross-pressures to the internal politics of interest groups, and observed that "felt conflicts of this sort are painful." In *The Congressional Party: A Case Study* (New York: John Wiley & Sons, 1959), p. 95, Truman implied that legislative

parties, as "mediate groups," shared many typical group characteristics.

20. A comparison of these distributions on the Fisher Exact Probability Test shows a difference significant at the .025 level of confidence.

21. Truman, *The Congressional Party*, pp. 193-95.

22. *Ibid.*, chaps. iv and vi.

23. Like so much else in political science, this is the type of proposition that requires elaboration to be accurate. Party voting in state legislatures is highest in two-party competitive states, lowest in one-party southern states and states with fragmented though equal parties, such as California. For a good discussion of the range of performance on this variable, see Fred I. Greenstein, *The American Party System and the American People* (Englewood Cliffs, N. J.: Prentice-Hall, 1963), chap. v; Thomas R. Dye, "State Legislative Politics," in *Politics in the American States: A Comparative Analysis,* ed. Herbert Jacob and Kenneth N. Vines (Boston: Little, Brown & Co., 1965), pp. 151–206; and Malcolm E. Jewell, *The State Legislature: Politics and Practice* (New York: Random House, 1962), chap. iii.

24. Duane Lockard, *New England State Politics* (Princeton: Princeton University Press, 1959), p. 217.

25. Wahlke *et al.*, "American State Legislators' Role Orientations," p. 226.

CHAPTER V

1. For general descriptions of New England Democratic parties, see Murray B. Levin with George Blackwood, *The Compleat Politician: Political Strategy in Massachusetts* (Indianapolis: Bobbs-Merrill Co., 1962), and Duane Lockard, *New England State Politics* (Princeton: Princeton University Press, 1959).

2. See Seymour M. Lipset, Martin A. Trow, and James S. Coleman, *Union Democracy: The Internal Politics of the International Typographical Union* (Glencoe, Ill.: Free Press, 1956), pp. 9–11.

3. For descriptions of the rise of the governorships, see Leslie Lipson, *The American Governor from Figurehead to Leader* (Chicago: University of Chicago Press, 1939), and Coleman R. Ransone, Jr., *The Office of the Governor in the United States* (University, Ala.: University of Alabama Press, 1956).

4. See Jay S. Goodman, "The Development of the Office of the Governor in Rhode Island" (Research Report No. I, Rhode Island Constitutional Convention, 1965), and Erwin L. Levine, *Theodore Francis Green: The Rhode Island Years, 1906–1936* (Providence: Brown University Press, 1963), chap. ix.

5. Lockard, *New England State Politics*, p. 205.

CHAPTER VI

1. Erwin L. Levine, *Theodore Francis Green: The Rhode Island Years, 1906–1936* (Providence: Brown University Press, 1963), chap. i.

2. See Murray Stedman, Jr., and Susan W. Stedman, "The Rise of the Democratic Party of Rhode Island," *New England Quarterly*, XXIV (1951), 331, 340.

3. Stedman and Stedman, "The Rise of the Democratic Party of Rhode Island," p. 331, and Duane Lockard, *New England State Politics* (Princeton: Princeton University Press, 1959), pp. 173–77.

4. John P. Hackett, "AFL-CIO Board Backs Gallogly," *Providence Journal*, October 22, 1964.

5. *Providence Journal*, October 23, 1964.

6. *Ibid.*, November 8, 1964.

7. John P. Hackett, "Sen. Sgambato Almost Fails to Get Labor Nod," *ibid.*, October 8, 1966; *Providence Journal*, November 3, 1966.

8. *Ibid.*, November 6, 1966.

9. *Ibid.*, February 1, 1967.

10. *Ibid.*, February 22, 1967.

11. *Ibid.*, April 7, 1967.

12. See Harmon Zeigler, *Interest Groups in American Society* (Englewood Cliffs, N. J.: Prentice-Hall, 1964), pp. 152–61, and Solomon Barkin, *The Decline of the Labor Movement and What Can Be Done About It* (Santa Barbara, Calif.: Center for the Study of Democratic Institutions, 1961).

13. See Philip Converse *et al.*, "Stability and Change in 1960: A Reinstating Election," *American Political Science Review*, LV (1961), 269–80, and "Electoral Myth and Reality: The 1964 Election," *American Political Science Review*, LIX (1965), 321–36, and Donald E. Stokes, "Some Dynamic Elements of Contests

for the Presidency," *American Political Science Review*, LX (1966), 19–28.

14. For a detailed explication of labor-union members' voting patterns, see Arthur Kornhauser, Harold L. Sheppard, and Albert J. Mayer, *When Labor Votes: A Study of Auto Workers* (New York: University Books, 1956), and V. O. Key, Jr., *Public Opinion and American Democracy* (New York: Alfred A. Knopf, 1961), pp. 521–22.

15. Much of what I have said about the behavior of the Rhode Island and national Democratic parties at the apogees of their strength appears to agree with the theories of William Riker in *The Theory of Political Coalitions* (New Haven: Yale University Press, 1962).

16. See Donald E. Stokes, "Analytic Reduction in the Study of Institutions," paper delivered at the 1966 Annual Convention of the American Political Science Association, New York, September 7–10, 1966.